BECOMING

A HEALING

PRESENCE

Albert S. Rossi, PhD

ANCIENT FAITH PUBLISHING ✝ CHESTERTON, INDIANA

Becoming a Healing Presence
© 2014 Albert S. Rossi

Published by:
   Ancient Faith Publishing
   A Division of Ancient Faith Ministries
   P.O. Box 748
   Chesterton, IN 46304

ISBN: 978-1-936270-16-3

Printed in the United States of America

20 19 18 17 16   13 12 11 10 9 8 7 6 5 4 3 2

Dr. Al Rossi is considered a treasure by seminarians and the many who have come to know him through retreats and podcasts. Now with *Becoming a Healing Presence* we have a written treasure as one more "gift from Al" that touches the soul and brings us ever closer to Christ our true physician and complete healer.

—Very Rev. Dr. Chad Hatfield, Chancellor, St. Vladimir's Seminary

Al Rossi's "little book" teaches you to go inward and find Jesus in the vast treasure house of your heart. Bits and pieces from family life interweave with sayings of the saints to take you on a journey that warms and equips your heart, sending you outward as a healing presence to others.

—Rev. Sarah L. Fogg, PhD, BCC, Palliative Care Chaplain

Dr. Rossi does here what most books on spirituality fail to do: he writes about how to live so as to be a healing presence in the messy world we inhabit today. He distills his decades of practical experience and thoughtful reflection living the Orthodox Christian way as a psychologist, university lecturer, seminary teacher, husband, father, and grandfather. His deceptively simple and accessible writing breathes with authenticity.

—V. Rev. Fr. John A. Jillions, Chancellor, OCA

Becoming a Healing Presence is a gift of calm to those caught up in the noise and busyness of our modern society. Through engaging personal stories, wisdom from the Church Fathers, and his professional experience as a clinical psychologist, Dr. Albert Rossi gently guides his readers toward prayerful stillness. His book is a peaceful and powerful reminder that to love is to foster healing in ourselves and in our neighbor through ceaseless communion with Christ. As one susceptible to becoming bound by earthly cares, I am very grateful for this curative dose of "the one thing needful."

—Molly Sabourin, author and podcaster, *Close to Home*

TO GAY, my eternal wife—though physically dead for decades, her vibrant spirit lives on. She is my strength and my song. She coauthored the book, guiding and guarding me through the more difficult passages. She is a model for all of us, a healing presence from her heavenly abode.

Contents

Foreword

A l Rossi and I can't recall exactly how I became his and his wife Gay's spiritual father and confessor. It happened when Gay was diagnosed with breast cancer that soon metastasized into bone cancer. Their spiritual father, who was also one of their closest personal friends, thought it would be best for me to take over his pastoral service at this crucial time. But how it actually worked itself out still remains a bit of a mystery to both of us.

I had seen the Rossi family many times at liturgical services and other events at St. Vladimir's Seminary (their home was a five-minute walk from the school), but my wife and I had not come to know them more than casually. I was serving a church in New York City around that time, and was also often away from the school, especially on weekends, attending to other duties.

It also happened about this same time that I was in charge of a retreat for young people at the seminary. Al had been invited to lead several sessions. At one of them he had the participants answer some questions and do certain exercises about their extended families, their childhood, their upbringing, their experience in the Church, their favorite films, books, music, etc. They did this in writing, just for themselves, to serve as a springboard to their discussions. They were not obliged to share with Al what they had written.

Being at the retreat, I decided to do what Al asked the participants to do. When I thanked Al at the end of the day for his good work, which I saw had a powerful impact on the young people, I handed him what I had written. "Have a look at this," I asked him, "and, if you wish, tell me what you think of it."

A few days later, I met Al on the seminary campus. He told me that he'd read what I wrote and thought it would be helpful for us to talk about it, adding with a tantalizing smile, "but this time on my turf." I eagerly agreed and began visiting Al at his office once a week. Our regularly scheduled meetings went on for more than a year. Since then we have continued to meet, speak, work, and pray together in countless ways. We were each in dire need of what the other had to offer, and still are. And so was Gay. But little did we know at the time how much the two of us needed her, and still do, in our spiritual lives.

The compelling tasks facing us from the beginning of our work together were Al and Gay's marriage and Gay's struggle with excruciatingly painful bone cancer. Their family life was in dreadful condition. Gay was indescribably angry and unhappy, and so, in turn, was Al. Their kids were caught in the middle of

it. Their history, individually and together, was the most complicated and painful story I ever encountered. It was also, for me at
that time, the most incredible. I had virtually no understanding
of almost anything that either of them had been through from
their childhood and youth and life together, both before and
after they found themselves a married couple with two beautiful children in the Orthodox Church—which situation, despite
its many graces and joys, was itself hardly an easy, smooth, or
painless experience.

The one thing that bound Al and me together in the most
intimate spiritual communion was our devotion to God's Gospel in Jesus Christ as witnessed in the Church's Scriptures and
offered by God's grace to our living experience (fragile, flawed,
and sinful though we be) by Christ and the Holy Spirit in the
liturgical worship, sacramental life, doctrinal teachings, and
spiritual counsels of the saints of the Orthodox Church.

Gay Rossi's agonizing journey, and ours with her, by which
we were purified and illumined by God's grace, was in every way
a perfect example of the truth of the psalmist's exclamations:
"Before I was afflicted I went astray; but now I keep Thy Word.
. . . It is good for me that I was afflicted, that I might learn Thy
statutes. . . . If Thy law had not been my delight, I should have
perished in my afflictions. I will never forget Thy precepts, for
by them Thou hast given me life. I am Thine, save me!" (Psalm
119:67, 72, 92–94).

This book, *Becoming a Healing Presence*, tells a vivid story of going into one's heart to find Christ, and then going out from one's heart to allow Christ to heal others through us. I am grateful to have been part of the healing of Gay Rossi and the subsequent impact her healing had on Al and the writing of this little book. I would say that every word in the book you, the reader, are holding in your hands could have an impact on you to become more of a healing presence. If you read the book, you will come to see it for yourself—if you have eyes to see, ears to hear, a mind willing to understand, and a heart ready to obey.

As Gay was progressively being cleansed, illumined, and saved by God's grace through what she was suffering in flesh and spirit, she began to say, "I'm determined to die healthy." Because she achieved her goal by the Lord's power, she and Al became the healing presence they now are for those desiring to be healed who are ready to count the cost and pay the price for this precious gift of God in His Son Jesus and the Holy Spirit in the Church.

In our last conversation before she died, I asked Gay the most important questions. "Gay," I asked, "What do you now say about God?"

She replied simply, "I worship God."

And I went on, "And why do you do so?"

She responded, again so simply, "Because I have come to know love."

I then said to her, "And what about Al?"

Her answer was firm and clear: "I see Al veiled in light."

I was present when Gay fell asleep in the Lord. She was breathing laboriously, as dying people do. We were reading psalms. Or simply standing in silence. Sometimes someone said a few words. Then, without warning, I suddenly began to cry. This was not at all like me, as those who knew me then would surely testify. Shortly after I stopped weeping, which took some time, Gay breathed her last and gave her life to God.

Later Al said to me in regard to this unexpected incident at her deathbed, "You know, Father Tom, I just bet that Gay decided not to die until you wept."

I responded, "You know, Al, it would be just like her to do so."

I drove home from the hospital after Gay's death listening to Nana Mouskouri singing that it is only love that changes everything. How true this is! Yet we must all come to know by experience what, or more precisely, *who*, this Love is. Al and his Gay help us here to do so. How grateful we should be to them, and to our Lord, for the invaluable gift of this little book.

Protopresbyter Thomas Hopko
Dean Emeritus,
St. Vladimir's Orthodox Theological Seminary

Introduction

WE ARE ALL LONGING to become something noble, something elevated, something beyond our earthbound selves. We have been created to be "gods," enfleshed with Christlikeness, in the full sense of the word, children of the living God.

The abiding question is, "How?" How are we to become disposed to receive such nobility? One way is to take these words of Christ seriously: "'Love the LORD your God with all your heart . . . and your neighbor as yourself'" (Luke 10:27).

This little book will build on the assumption that the way we interact with our neighbors, both those close to us and those more remote, is the way we interact with Christ, with the living God.

Christ is everything. Christ is our Physician, our complete healer. He wants us to be His humanity on earth, His healing presence to others. We are a healing presence to others when we give them strength and when we give them hope.

> *St. Athanasius the Great said of St. Anthony, "Through him the Lord heals man." The statement is made in the present tense and pertains not only to St. Anthony but also to us.*

Of course, the foundational truth of the Christian life is a life of love. This little book tries to operationalize love in a *concrete* way. During our interactions with others, we know when we give them strength and hope. That is, we know when we empower them or when we diminish them. All we have to do is observe them as we interact and then watch the way they walk afterward.

The thesis of this book is that we are all called to be a healing presence to others, always. When we are a healing presence to others, we are, in some sense, a healing presence to Christ Himself, who resides in others. Better said, Christ is the healing presence in us who moves through us to heal others.

CHAPTER I

Inner Stillness

···

O N AN AIRPLANE, as a flight prepares to depart, the flight
attendant tells the passengers that, in case of an emergency, oxygen bags will drop from overhead. Those passengers
with infants will receive two masks. The adult is to put his or
her own oxygen mask on first, and only then put a mask on
the infant.

For me, as an Italian grandfather, those instructions are
counterintuitive. I want to give my life for my grandchild, to care
for her first, and then myself. But—and this is a big but—if I
truly love my granddaughter, I will put my own oxygen mask on
first, then hers. The sequence is vital to my granddaughter's survival. If I don't take care of myself first, both of us might be lost.

The oxygen mask example is a model for becoming a healing presence to others. If I don't take care of myself first, I have
nothing to give to others. People seek me out as a counselor
and expect that when they come into my office, I have time
and energy for them. They don't need a tired, grumpy, sleep-

deprived, inattentive, and self-absorbed counselor. The only way I can have something to give is if I have allowed Christ to care for me first and foremost. There is no other way.

I begin to care for myself by centering my being, my soul-mind-body. I allow Christ to center me by gradually becoming still inwardly, which is no small task in today's environment.

Stillness Is a Choice

OUR ELDERS TELL US that the person seeking inner stillness is someone who has embarked upon the journey into his own heart—not someone who shuts himself off physically from others, but someone who "returns into himself," closing the door of his mind. Solitude is a state of soul, not a matter of geographical location, and the real desert lies within the heart. As St. Basil said, we return to ourselves; and having returned inwardly, we ascend to God.[1]

What kind of journey does the Christian take? To be a Christian is to be a sojourner, for spiritually we are always on the move. We are on a journey through the inward space of the heart, a journey not measured by the hours of our watch or the days on the calendar, for it is a journey out of time into eternity. The seeker begins to wait upon God in stillness and silence,

---

1   Kallistos Ware, *The Inner Kingdom* (Crestwood, NY: SVS Press, 2000), p. 93.

no longer talking about God or to God but simply listening. We could say the person who is seeking stillness is seeking to become a healing presence for others.

Exterior silence is a prelude to inner silence. We can't be wrapped in a noisy fog and expect to attain inner stillness. Silence is a free choice. Yet the only freedom we have is to say, "Thy will be done," or "My will be done." So our free choice is to want the Lord's will and be open to the silence He provides.

> *Silence is a free choice.*

Silence doesn't just happen out of nowhere. Rather, the opposite usually happens. When we least expect it, noise of all sorts can appear from nowhere.

Here is an example from my own life. When my son, Timothy, was in high school, he was on the golf team and often played in tournaments. I was his chauffeur. Sometimes the tournaments were ninety miles away. While I was driving, Tim would turn on the radio to his favorite music station, Z100. It was not outrageous music but certainly not to my taste.

One day it dawned on me that I was being held captive by my son's music choices. So I said to him, "Tim, do you know what? The radio in the car is half mine. You listen to what you want for half of our trips, and I'll listen to what I want for the other half. How does that sound?"

He replied, "Oh sure, Dad, that's fair."

As we prepared for a long drive, I said, "So, Tim, do you

want to hear your music going to the tournament or coming back?" Like a typical teenager he said, in effect, "I'll take my jollies now."

After the tournament, we started the drive home. It was seven-thirty in the evening, and Tim was a little tired but pleasant. He took off his golf shoes and prepared to relax. Instantly he reached for the radio. I said, "Whoa, Tim, my turn to use the radio."

"Oh yeah, Dad, what station would you like?"

"I'll use my radio time to leave the radio turned off, please."

"Okay," he said. But for the next hour and a half, he squirmed and restlessly turned in the front seat. He scratched the ceiling, put his feet on the dashboard, and made circles on the side window. He was agitated.

I love my boy and wouldn't do anything to hurt him. Really, I simply wanted some time of silence in the car.

Interestingly, now that he is an adult, he says to me, "Dad, some of the best times we had together were the drives back from golf tournaments." I suppose that, while in the car, he had to release his pent-up adolescent energy by tossing about. But beneath the writhing exterior, he was, in some sense, enjoying the silence. Together we could watch the sun setting and enjoy the early evening restfulness. I also think Timothy learned a valuable lesson on those drives back, although that wasn't my purpose in keeping the radio off. I kept the radio off to retain my sanity.

In *Living Prayer*, Metropolitan Anthony Bloom wrote, "The Greek Fathers set this silence, which they called *hesychia*, both as the starting-point and the final achievement of prayer." What does this silence look like? Silence is a way, a state of soul, in which all the powers of the soul and the faculties of the body are completely at peace, quiet, and recollected, perfectly alert yet free from any turmoil or agitation.[2]

In the *Philokalia*, St. Hesychios tells us about this opening to divine mystery, increased intimacy with Christ through contemplation, "It activates the soul to penetrate the divine and hidden mysteries and leads us, as far as this is possible, to a sure knowledge of the inapprehensible God."[3]

Is contemplation rather rare among Orthodox Christians today? Of course, I don't know. But based on my limited experience talking about the personal spiritual journey with good-willed Christians, I would concur with St. Hesychios's assessment from ages gone by. On the matter of daily and serious quiet time for prayer, I think we all have a long way to go. And there is no better place to start than here. No better time to start than now.

Of course, this opens many questions. How *do* we deepen

---

2   Anthony Bloom, *Living Prayer* (Springfield, IL: Templegate Publishers, 1966), p. 110.

3   Hesychios the Priest, "On Watchfulness and Holiness," in G.E.H. Palmer, Philip Sherrard, and Kallistos Ware, trans. and eds., *The Philokalia: The Complete Text*, vol. I (London & Boston: Faber & Faber, 1979), pp. 162–163.

our inner stillness? How do stillness and prayer go together? And what is the role of prayer in healing?

The Language of Stillness

WHERE DO WE BEGIN to put the oxygen mask on ourselves first? We begin where the Scriptures tell us to begin. We begin with outer and inner stillness.

Stillness speaks, sometimes clearly and sometimes "through a glass darkly." We know that Psalm 46:10 tells us, "Be still, and know that I *am* God." The converse is implied: If I am not still, I run the danger of not knowing the real God. If I don't know God, I don't know myself, because I am made in God's image and likeness. I need to know God to know who I am, to have an authentic identity. Much of the contemporary search for identity is a deeper, though often unconscious, seeking for Christ within our hearts.

As Aleksandr Solzhenitsyn said, not everything has a name. Some things lead us into a realm beyond words.

In Isaiah 30:15 we find a clear rebuke from God: "For thus says the Lord GOD, the Holy One of Israel [when the Lord God is mentioned twice, the emphasis means that what follows is important], 'In returning and rest you shall be saved; in quietness [stillness] and confidence shall be your strength." God's request of the people is the same request He made of Moses:

rest and quietness—that is, stillness. And the next four words in Isaiah are devastating to the Israelites, and to us: "But you would not." Would not what? Would not be still. "And you said, 'No, for we will flee on horses. . . . We will ride on swift *horses.*'"

We, too, refuse to be still. We say, in effect, "No! I need to go on the internet and my smartphone. I need to work on my many good projects. I need to talk with friends and plan good things. I will schedule my day with beneficial projects and even church-related work. But, Lord, I'll tell you one thing: I will not be still." Okay, but we pay a high price for not being still.

We are back to silence being a choice, as led by God. When my daughter was a teenager, she had a sign outside her bedroom door. The sign said, "Everyone is entitled to my opinion." That may be the way teens think. Beth is now married and living on the other side of the equation. She has learned to be quiet and is trying to raise her three energetic children to value silence. We learn as we grow.

The high price for not being still is the possibility that we might not know God. If we don't know God, we don't know ourselves, because we are made in God's image and likeness. That's who we are. Hence, today many people are looking for their identity, for their place in the world, for who they are. The only place we can find who we are is in God.

The only person to respond perfectly to God's desire for stillness was Jesus hanging on the Cross. He did what the Israelites of old refused to do. He did what we often refuse to do.

And, in that act of supreme stillness, He saved the cosmos.

We need to seek silence so we can begin to be still. Elders tells us that unless we maintain contact with our inner depths, unless there is a *still center* in the middle of the storm, unless in the middle of all our activity we preserve a secret space in our heart where we stand alone with God, we will lose all sense of direction and be torn in pieces. All of us must, to the extent that we can, be hermits of the heart.

How Synergy Operates

WE MUST COOPERATE WITH GRACE. All the good is from Christ. Yet, in the deep mystery of synergy, we have a strategic part to play.

I am reminded of the story of the six-year-old boy who went to the department store with his dad to buy a Christmas present for his mother. The dad said, "I think Mom would like slippers for Christmas. What do you think? Let's go to the slipper department. Mom likes pink, fluffy slippers. What do you think? Mom takes size six. What size do you want to get?" The boy kept repeating, "Yes." So the boy pointed to a pair of women's pink, fluffy slippers, size six. The dad paid the sales clerk, and they went home.

Dad got out the wrapping paper, Scotch tape, and scissors. The boy put tape on the paper that Dad cut and folded. And on Christmas, the boy rightly told his mother that he got her the Christmas present of his choice. The mother was thrilled that her son was so thoughtful and had picked out the perfect Christmas gift for her.

It was the boy who chose the slippers and gave them to his mother. And the boy was guided and empowered by his father. We might say the father was the prime mover in the Christmas present choice. In a sense, so it is with us. We know we have strengthened another human, and we know that Christ did it within us.

So, a healing presence is, in a sense, a conduit of fire. The fire of the Godhead, hotter than the sun, goes through the clay conduit, us, and out the other side as fire to another human. We simply allow the fire to go through us. But it is a healing fire nonetheless. Fire goes into us and out from us to heal the wounds of someone else. Of course, the conduit is put aside afterward, empty and hollow, but it was and can again be very useful to Christ to do His loving work for others. We, the conduit, must accept the place of Christ's healing power through us.

Here is a story that is difficult for me to relate but may be helpful in understanding our part in this synergy. Poachers in Africa catch monkeys by hollowing out a coconut shell and making a small hole in the front of the shell, just large enough for the monkey to scrunch its hand through. In the back of the coconut shell, the poachers bore a small hole, tighten an eye bolt into it, put a chain through the hole in the bolt, and lock the chain around the bottom of a tree. They fill the shell with a mixture of pineapple and rice—delectable morsels for monkeys. Then the poachers go home.

A monkey comes, forces its hand through the opening in the coconut, and grabs a fistful of pineapple and rice. Now, however, it can't pull its hand back out because of its large fist. But the monkey will simply not let go of the food. It stubbornly retains its grip. The poachers return the next morning, put a bag over the monkey, chop off its hand, and return home to make monkey soup. The story, though true, is grim for the monkey. And, in a sense, we are all monkeys, not letting go of our resistance to stillness and more life. We refuse to be still.

We can learn from the monkey story and learn to let go to be still. When we are still, we walk through the semi-permeable membrane separating us from the inner universe within us. We can almost walk through that membrane and "be there"—be in faith with the Lord Jesus.

Stillness Opens Us to Prayer

IN HIS BOOKLET *The Power of the Name*, Metropolitan Kallistos Ware writes:

> When you pray you yourself must be silent. . . . You must be silent; let the prayer speak. Silence is not merely negative—a pause between words—but highly positive; it is an attitude of attentive alertness, of vigilance, and above all of listening. The

*person who prays is the one who listens to the voice of prayer in
his own heart, and he understands that this voice is not his own
but that of Another speaking within him.*[4]

So, what happens when we are still? We can begin to listen to
the voice of God.

When we say the name Jesus, we are both speaking and listening. How do we listen *as* we speak? Therein lies the great
mystery of divine communication. God speaks to us in His own
intonation, His own coloration, His own harmonious sound.

What happens if we try to become more still and pray, even
a little more? St. John Chrysostom said if we try to pray more,
we "rouse the snake within us."

Then how can we learn to stop talking and to start listening? Instead of simply speaking to God, how can we make our
own the prayer in which God speaks to us? One way to embark
on this journey inward is through the invocation of the Name.

We are interested in getting closer to God. But according
to St. Isaac of Syria, it is impossible to draw near to God by any
means other than increasing prayer.

Then we assess the size of the task of prayer. And we find
that the task is beyond difficult. Abba Agathon said, "To pray is
the hardest of all tasks." If we do not find prayer difficult, perhaps it is because we have not really started to pray.

---

4   Kallistos Ware, *The Power of the Name* (Fairacres, Oxford, UK: SLG
    Press, 1986.

Contemplation as Transformation

SPIRITUAL AUTHORS TELL US that we need to spend some time every day being still, either seated or standing. They encourage us to have a "prayer word"—the Jesus Prayer, the single name "Jesus," some other short prayer, or silence. Our quest for a spiritual life pivots on quiet time and intimacy with Christ. Our quiet time can be part of our personal prayer rule as directed by our spiritual father.

The usual directive is to sit attentively for a period of time every day. *Every* day. In his fine little booklet, *The Power of the Name*, Metropolitan Kallistos says that the Jesus Prayer, or a variant of it, "causes the brightness of the Transfiguration to penetrate into every corner of our life." He goes on to say that if we spend a few moments in contemplation every day, "we deepen and transform the remaining moments of the day, rendering ourselves available to others, effective and creative in a way that we could not otherwise be."

So we are called to be faithful to our rule of quiet time with the Lord every day, faithful to the Word dwelling in us, faithful to a steadfast call of God that we may "ask, and it will be given to [us]; seek, and [we] will find; knock, and it will be opened [to us]" (Matt. 7:7). Choosing a time to be quiet with Christ, a time of contemplation, is our part in the synergy between God and us.

Some people are able to spend twenty minutes in the morning and twenty minutes in the evening, sitting quietly, saying their prayer word. Other people have less time to spend in quiet contemplation. The answer is not arithmetic. Quantity is not primary. Steadfastness in choosing to be still, every day, is primary.

What can we expect if we decide to sit quietly for a period of time every day? We learn that when we get quiet, our dark inner world explodes out. All the repressed negative thoughts, all the undone tasks, all the backed-up sludge comes to the surface. That's ugly. So we just stay busy and avoid the discomfort. But if we allow that phase to pass—and it will pass—a gradual peace floods our soul. St. John Chrysostom said that if we continue to pray, we "lay the snake low." What beautiful phraseology! We become conquerors. This is a scene of conquest. We gradually begin to allow the light of Christ in, and a gradual expansion of consciousness occurs.

> *Contemplation is a gift we receive, not a program we design.*

However, like faith, contemplation is a gift we receive, not a program we design. God's ways often seem serendipitous. During quiet time, we may experience mostly serenity or mostly dryness. Whatever. It was said that Teresa of Avila, the great Roman Catholic saint who founded the Discalced Carmelites, said that for long stretches of time her quiet prayer was spent "counting the grains of sand as they fell through the hourglass."

That is to say, she experienced long periods of dryness during prayer time. Many of the great saints tell of extended bouts of this dryness.

We enter our quiet time of contemplation with no expectations except to put ourselves in God's hands. He does with us as He will. We don't expect lower cholesterol, stabilized blood pressure, or a sunny outlook. But we can expect more intimacy with Christ, however that occurs.

Our role is simply to be as still as possible and to pray as best we can, faithfully. God provides the rest.

> *We become a healing presence by becoming still.*

We trust in God to give us what we need. The soldiers in the Revolutionary War had a saying: "Trust in God and keep your powder dry." Our war is not against other humans. Rather, it is with ourselves. We keep our "powder dry" by doing our part, by choosing to be still. The spiritual war rages, and we can be victorious.

CHAPTER 2

Breathing the Name Jesus

As we try to become still, what do we do? The Fathers suggest that we begin by becoming aware of our breathing. We go gently inside.

> *God is breath.*

As the sixth-century monk St. John Climacus said in *The Ladder of Divine Ascent*, in the chapter "A Brief Summary of All the Preceding Steps," "Let the remembrance of Jesus be present with your every breath. Then indeed you will appreciate the value of stillness."[5] St. Maximus said simply that God is breath. And Philotheos stated, "We must always breathe God."

In our silence we try to become centered. As St. Ignatius Brianchaninov recommends in his book *On the Jesus Prayer*, we

---

5   John Climacus, *The Ladder of Divine Ascent* (Mahwah, NJ: Paulist Press, 1982), p. 270.

try to be aware of our "quiet steady breathing." He goes on to say, "Breathe with care, gently and slowly."

This all may seem basic, but in today's culture and probably in our own lives, it isn't easy. When my wife and I took the children camping, I was amazed at the campground scene in the early evening. After supper and the dishes were cleaned, many families went into their tent for "family time in the woods." Many of those tents had a portable TV, and families sat in those tents watching what they would have watched at home. Hmmm. When we went downhill skiing and appreciated the sights and sounds of the majestic mountain, many other skiers had their trusty iPods along so they could listen to whatever they listened to in their usual lives. Hmmm. We are all tempted to squash silence one way or another. I am not immune to such diversions.

> *Let us utter the name of Jesus as often as we breathe. For it is light to our darkened mind. The guarding of the mind is rightly and worthily called light-giving, producer of light, source of light, and bearer of fire.*
>
> *We should always be turning the name of Jesus Christ around the spaces of our heart as lightning circles around the skies before rain.*[6]

---

6   E. Kadloubovsky and G. E. H. Palmer, trans., *Writings from the Philokalia on Prayer of the Heart* (London: Faber & Faber, 1961), p. 300.

The Name as Breath

WHAT DO WE BREATHE? We breathe the name of Jesus. His Person is mysteriously encapsulated in His name. His name is His Presence. "I will strengthen them in the LORD, and they shall walk up and down in His Name" (Zech. 10:12).

We are told in the Bible, "And whatever you do in word or deed, *do* all in the name of the Lord Jesus" (Col. 3:17).

We just breathe His name. As Father Lev Gillet suggests, we "let the Name penetrate our soul—as a drop of oil spreads out and impregnates a cloth. Let nothing of yourself escape. Surrender your whole self and enclose it within the Name."[7]

I illustrated this quotation during a class I taught at St. Vladimir's Seminary. During the class, I recited the quotation and put a piece of linen cloth on the desk. Then I put a drop of oil on the cloth. The seminarians and I looked at the single, tan spot of oil on the white cloth. Near the end of class, I picked up the cloth to show the students how the spot had disappeared into the cloth. The white linen had become slightly olive-colored throughout. The "spot" became the entire cloth. That's the way the name of Jesus penetrates our souls and bodies.

Many Orthodox spiritual writers say that one way to embark on this journey inward is through the invocation of the name "Lord Jesus." They say this isn't the only way, but it

---

7   Lev Gillet, *On the Invocation of the Name of Jesus* (Springfield, IL: Templegate Publishers, 1985), p. 30.

> St. Ignatius Brianchaninov said, "Breathe with care, gently and slowly."

is a way of utmost simplicity.

According to Father Gillet, "The Name itself is a means of purification, a touchstone, a filter through which our thoughts, words, and deeds have to pass to be freed from their impurities. None of them ought to be admitted by us until we pass them through the Name—and the Name excludes all sinful elements." And, he continues, "This is a severe asceticism. It requires a forgetfulness of self, a dying to self as the Holy Name grows in our soul."

Popular bookstores are replete with books on living in the present moment. What does that really mean? When we live in the present moment, are we alone with the moment of awareness—or is there more?

We breathe with care, gently and slowly. The gentle repetition of the name may be likened to the beating of wings by which a bird rises into the air. The breathing and repetition of the name must never be labored or forced, hurried, or in the nature of flapping. Rather, it must be gentle, easy, and—let us give the word its deepest meaning—graceful. When the bird has reached its desired height, it glides effortlessly in flight. It beats its wings only from time to time to remain aloft. So, too, with us. When we attain an awareness of Jesus, then we say His holy name intermittently to keep us focused on Him. The repetition is resumed only when other thoughts threaten to crowd out the awareness of the Lord.[8]

In *On the Invocation of the Name of Jesus*, Father Gillet says, "Let us not regard our prayer in relation to fulfillment in the future but in relation to fulfillment in Jesus now. Jesus is more than the giver of what others and we need. He is both giver and gift, containing in Himself all good things." And he adds, "The Name of Jesus brings victory and peace when we are tempted."

The Voice of God

As we slow down to hear our breathing, we can become aware of an inner vastness opening up, a new dimension to our awareness. This is the beginning of an awareness of the holy presence of God. Within that space we can become alert to God guiding and strengthening us, aware of His voice. We slowly become aware of Him as our strength and our song.

When I first began to give retreats in Orthodox churches, I gave one in Washington, D.C. After speaking for a while on the topic of God's voice, I gave the participants index cards and asked them to describe an experience they'd had of "hearing the voice of God," not with their ears but with an inner intuition that God was mysteriously making His presence known.

---

8   Gillet, *On the Invocation*, p. 21.

I had never done such an exercise with an Orthodox group and had misgivings, thinking the approach might be too evangelical or too demanding. To my surprise, all the participants began writing energetically, and I heaved a sigh of relief. When they finished, I asked if anyone wanted to share what they had written. A young priest in the back shot up his hand. I asked him to come up to the front and share his notes.

He began with a sentence I will never forget: "I heard God's voice in a PathMark [a large grocery chain]." I knew one thing at that moment. I knew I had never heard God's voice in a Path-Mark, although I had been shopping in one many times.

The priest went on to say that, while he was standing in the checkout line, the woman in front of him gave her eleven-year-old daughter a dollar and pointed to the homeless man standing by the door. The girl went to the homeless man, gave him the dollar, and came back to her mother. The mother shook her head, whispered something in the girl's ear, and again pointed to the homeless man. The girl went to the man, gave him a hug, and returned to her mother. Her mother then gave her a hug. The priest said he heard God telling him that this was the way he ought to treat poor people.

> "But blessed are your eyes, for they see, and your ears for they hear."
> (Matthew 13:16)

That scene could happen to any of us. A mother teaches her daughter a lesson in loving outreach. Period. And what a lovely lesson for the daughter and the bystanders to learn! However, the priest was making an extravagant claim. He was claiming that, for him, it was not a lesson in altruism but an experience of God speaking directly to him through the actions of the mother and daughter. The priest's interpretation is that of faith, which makes all the difference.

We can see our experiences through the eyes of nature—as acts of altruism—or through the eyes of faith—as God's voice, as the priest had. Perhaps that is what the Lord meant when He said, "But blessed *are* your eyes, for they see, and your ears for they hear" (Matt. 13:16). Are we growing in our ability to see and hear God's voice in daily life?

Life as a Treasure Hunt

SOMETIMES THE LORD PROVIDES wisdom in the unlikeliest of circumstances. I was at a convention, sitting in a small conference room listening to a speaker, when she spoke a sentence that struck my heart: "Life is like a treasure hunt." Somehow I knew she had something special to say to me. She went on to say that she had received three treasures from God that day, and it was early in the afternoon. She recounted her treasures, and they were ordinary. Yet as she perceived them, they were extraordinary. She said we have only to seek to find the treasures God has hidden for us in our day.

As an aside, right now as I was typing, I stopped to check my email. A woman wrote that she would be coming to my office soon. She attached a photo of her three-year-old son asleep. For me, the attached photo became a small treasure, sent as a gift from God. I could see the boy's sweetly closed eyes as the eyes of an angel, an innocent angelic boy. So life is a treasure hunt for us, wanting us to actively pursue with the eyes of faith the gifts that God is placing in our path.

After that convention, I was passing through airport security. An older man, a TSA employee, checked my bag and asked how my day was going. Intuitively, I knew he had a soft soul. I asked, "Can I tell you a quick anecdote?" He said, "Sure."

So I told him the little story of the woman at the convention. Then he looked me in the eye for a few seconds and said, "You just made my day." His reply made my day, too, of course. It was a hidden treasure, a gift from God to me. And that short exchange, years ago, remains as a treasure in my trove of memories. It became significant enough to include in this book.

Isn't the claim "Life is a treasure hunt" a contemporary interpretation of Matthew 13:44: "the kingdom of heaven is like treasure hidden in a field, which a man found and hid; and for joy over it he goes and sells all that he has and buys that field." The man found the treasure in a field, and knowing that he now possessed a treasure, he was filled with joy. So, too, with us. We can actively look for treasures during our day, perceive them as gifts from God, lovingly given to us, and "sell all that we have"— that is, put aside other interpretations of the events—and see them through the eyes of faith.

Treasures come in large and small packages. For example, God gave me a large treasure from my seven-year-old grandson, Collin, when I least expected it.

My daughter, Beth, along with her husband, their three little children, and I went to Divine Liturgy, followed by an extended coffee hour. As we drove home, the rain was pouring outside, but inside the van we were comfortable. Beth and Greg sat in the front seat, the two small children were in the middle seat, and Collin and I were in the far back seat. With the downpour, Collin and I seemed to have a private room in the back. No one could hear us, and we had fun playing with my smartphone. I asked if he would like to hear his voice on the phone. He sang "Happy Birthday" to my answering machine at home. I then redialed and let him listen to his voice. He giggled. We talked for a while. Then we were quiet, silently listening to the rain on the roof.

Suddenly Collin turned in his car seat, leaned toward me, and asked in a semi-adult voice, "Poppa, who do you love more: God or me?" I groaned inwardly. I didn't need a teaching moment when I felt so comfortable and so cushy. But there we were. His eyes were fixed on mine, and he was expecting a direct answer. I knew he didn't want to hear, "I love both of you," or some extended explanation. His was a simple question needing a straightforward answer.

By God's grace, I shrugged my shoulders, leaned toward him, and said softly, "God." He seemed satisfied, and we rode the rest of the way home in contented silence. Only later did I realize that Collin's question was, in effect, God's question to Abraham: "Abraham, whom do you love more, your family or Me?"

I've told that story to many people. Some say, "Oh, he's too young. I would have said I love Collin more than anything." But I know I would say the same thing again. I think Collin deserved to hear what his poppa believes, unvarnished and unequivocal.

Those God-given opportunities provide much material for the future. A few months later I was in bed with Collin, and I asked if he remembered the exchange. He said, "Oh sure, Poppa." He recounted the entire story.

I said, "Collin, if you don't mind, I'll now ask you, who do you love more, God or Poppa?" His eyes went out of focus, and I knew the question was beyond him. He didn't want to disappoint Poppa by saying God, yet he didn't know what he was really being asked.

Together we can teach each other about choosing God above all.

In his confusion, Collin asked the perfect question: "Poppa, what do you want me to say?" He wanted me to provide him with the right answer. Sweet little boy.

I softly said, "God."

He then followed with an obedient answer. "Well then, I'll say God."

I don't think Collin had much of an idea what was going on, but he was cooperative and willingly learning from his poppa.

Needless to say, I will revisit that exchange with Collin and his younger brother and sister in the months and years to come. Together we can teach each other about choosing God above all.

Memory and Breath

HUMAN MEMORY IS DEEPLY FLAWED and fallible. Psychologists tell us that most memories are negative. Once I gave my psychology class an informal experiment. I asked them to write their first memory anonymously on an index card. I collected the cards and discussed the results with the class. By far, most of the memories were painfully negative. The students' statements included, "I flushed my dad's wallet down the toilet when I was three," and "I broke my arm when I fell out of a tree." Very few were positive memories, and those were rather superficial, like "My earliest memory is my birthday party." We could speculate about the reasons for this, such as living in the fallen state, but the fact remains that our memory is bent toward darkness.

We humans tend to attribute more certainty to our own memory than to actual fact. When asked to give a metaphor for memory, most people suggest a computer or a camera or a digital recorder. We think our memory is a storehouse of valid, static information, rather like a computer's memory. However, that is simply not the case. Memory consists of encoded chemicals that continually change.

Experiments show that a person can write a memory of an event, with details, and be certain of the facts. A few months later, the same person can be asked to recount the same event with the same details and will give a slightly different version. However, the person is just as sure the second time that the new version is the same as the old version and that the memory is incontestable. In effect, the person is saying, "That is my experience. I know what I experienced, and no one can argue with my subjective experience and my memory of the events. It is mine, and who can argue with me?"

Humility provides an antidote to a prideful belief that our mind can think and remember with certainty. Without God, we can do nothing good, not even remember properly.

The awareness of our thought patterns and memory provides a platform for continual prayer. And our breath gives us the opportunity to remember Christ, not our thoughts and meandering memories. Along with St. John Climacus in his Step 27, "On Stillness," we can say, "Let the remembrance of Jesus be present with your every breath. Then indeed you will appreciate the value of stillness."[9]

Without humility and some attempt to remember Jesus,

---

9   Climacus, *Ladder of Divine Ascent*, p. 270.

the results of comparing memories of the same event become predictable. Two people, especially a married couple, can have the same experience but retain somewhat different memories of the details. If each insists his or her version is the only version, then any challenge becomes an attack on that person's veracity. That spells distance and division between the couple. Sometimes it spells a major argument.

The healing of memories begins with the admission that memory is flawed and changes with time. Left to our own devices—that is, our stream of consciousness and our memories—we can easily become dark and despondent.

We become a healing presence to ourselves by remembering Jesus, as St. John Climacus recommends, and by preserving the joy we have in the present moment. We become a healing presence to others as we try to help them see how memories don't have to control them or paralyze them. Memories, like all of life, can be given to Jesus and transformed into His joy in us.

Breath and Prayer

ONE OF THE BEST definitions of prayer is simply "communication with God." Never let it be said that prayer is easy. Rather, prayer is

> *Let the remembrance of Jesus be present with your every breath.*

a dangerous adventure, and we cannot enter it without risk.[10]

The problem is one of praying attentively, simply, and truthfully without replacing the real God with a false God, an idol, or a product of our imagination, and without trying to have a mystical experience.[11]

St. Ignatius Brianchaninov tells us:

> It is of the nature of inner prayer to reveal the hidden passions concealed in the human heart and to tame them. Inner prayer shows us our captivity to the fallen spirits, making us realize our imprisonment and freeing us from it. . . . At times the onset of passions and the invasion of hostile thoughts are so powerful that it leads to a great struggle in the soul. This is the time of hidden martyrdom.[12]

> *Every prayer changes the entire cosmos.*

Prayer changes me, not necessarily the situation. Yet, paradoxically, every prayer changes the entire cosmos. We live with that paradox and pray as best we can.

Once I took a group of students to visit a shelter for pregnant, unwed women. A celibate, unmarried woman directed the shelter. It was a haven for the pregnant women, and the woman who directed the shelter seemed to be

---

10 Anthony Bloom, *Living Prayer* (Springfield, IL: Templegate Publishers, 1996), p. 9.

11 Ibid., pp. 108-109.

12 Chariton of Valamo, comp., *The Art of Prayer* (London: Faber & Faber, 1977), p. 216.

a saint. My students were amazed by the care and hospitality they saw. During the question-and-answer session at the end, one student asked, "With all the work you do here, how do you have time to pray?"

Without a blink, the director of the shelter said, "You have been here about an hour. I have prayed fifteen times during your visit." Enough said. The director prayed during her day, and it seems she prayed incessantly.

Breath as a Doorway

STILLNESS COUPLED WITH an awareness of our breathing gradually opens our minds to God, rather like a door opening to a new unfolding, an unfolding of the wonder of being loved.

We need silence to still the chaos of the mind. As St. Gregory Palamas said, "That is why some teachers recommend beginners to pay attention to the exhalation and inhalation of their breath, and to restrain it a little, so that while they are watching the breathing, the intellect, too, may be held in check." Really, we are all beginners.

As we become aware of the other Presence within us, we become attuned to the truth that we have something to give that can heal others. We become increasingly aware of becoming a healing presence to ourselves, and hence, to others as well.

CHAPTER 3

The Healing Heart

G OD PLACED OUR HEART in the center of our chest as a gift—a gift of a life-giving energy supply. We begin our reflection on our heart with Jesus' words, "For where your treasure is, there your heart will be also" (Matt. 6:21). Our heart is our treasure-house.

What are we to do with this insight? St. Isaac said we dive into our physical heart to then enter the spiritual heart, the inner universe. He said,

> Enter eagerly into the treasure house that is within you, and so you will see the things that are of heaven—for there is but one single entry to them both. The ladder that leads to the Kingdom is hidden within your soul. Flee from sin, dive into yourself, and in your soul you will discover the stairs by which to ascend.[13]

St. Isaac the Syrian's purpose is to assure us that there exists, hidden within each one of us, a secret treasure-house, an

---

13 Kallistos Ware, *The Inner Kingdom* (Crestwood, NY: SVS Press, 2000), p. xi.

inner kingdom, that is amazing in its depth and variety. It is a place of wonder and joy, a place of glory, a place of encounter and dialogue. If only we will dive into ourselves, then we will each discover eternity within our own heart.

> St. Theophan the Recluse said, "The essence of the Christian life consists in establishing oneself with the mind in the heart before God."

Jacob's ladder starts from the very point where I am at this moment; the gate of heaven is everywhere. And this inner kingdom, present within me here and now, is at the same time the Kingdom of the age to come. The same path leads simultaneously to both of them.

St. Theophan the Recluse wrote in the classic *Unseen Warfare,*

The Homilies of St. Makarios develop this idea of the heart: "The heart governs and reigns over the whole bodily organism; and when grace possesses the ranges of the heart, it rules over all the members and the thoughts. For there, in the heart, is the mind, and all the thoughts of the soul and its expression [incredibly valid and foreseeing the discoveries of modern neurocardiology].... Within the heart are unfathomable depths. There are reception rooms and bedchambers in it, doors and porches, and many offices and passages. In it is the workshop of righteousness and of wickedness. In it is death; in it is life.... The heart is Christ's palace; there Christ the King comes to take His rest, with the angels and the spirits of the saints, He dwells there, walking within it and placing His Kingdom there."[14]

The healing heart is one that is a chapel for Jesus, for His Name to dwell in. The Name of Jesus is a burning light, acting as a lens or prism; it can gather and direct light until Fire (healing power) is kindled in us.

God's Heart Becomes Our Heart

IN THE BIBLE, God is presented as having a heart of His own. "But now your kingdom shall not continue. The LORD has sought for Himself a man after His own heart, and the LORD has commanded him *to be* commander over His people" (1 Sam. 13:14). And "He raised up for them David as king, to whom also He gave testimony and said, 'I have found David the *son* of Jesse, a man after My *own* heart, who will do all My will'" (Acts 13:22). God's heart is a heart of love.

We are made in God's image and likeness. His being, His heart becomes our heart to the extent that we are capable of opening ourselves to His divine life. As Alexander Solzhenitsyn wrote, "The battle line between good and evil runs through every human heart."

---

14 Nicodemus of the Holy Mountain, ed., and Theophan the Recluse, rev. ed., *Unseen Warfare* (Crestwood, NY: SVS Press, 1995), quoting *Philokalia*, pt. 1, p. 112.

The heart is where we heal or restore our baptismal grace. St. Gregory of Sinai said that we restore the grace of baptism through many labors in following the commandments and through a constant invocation of the Lord Jesus in prayer: "Let us have only this work of prayer in our heart, without forms, without images, till it warms our heart and makes it burn with ineffable love of the Lord."

One day when I was teaching at Pace University, I took a walk between classes along a path through the woods. At times the path would fork into two directions, meeting again further ahead. I asked God which path to take, left or right, as I continued walking. I heard no voice. I saw no direction sign. I didn't stop to wait for an answer. I simply walked as my heart directed. To this day I have no idea why the left route was better than the right path for me. But I do believe that somehow God is present in the smallest choices of our lives and, to the extent that we can, we need to include Him in the choices. So, on that day at Pace University, God was with me and preferred the left path for "us" to walk, even though I was apparently alone.

God's disclosures are not always clear. If we ask for guidance, we can grow in faith by believing that God answers the prayer, no matter how small or large the issue of the moment. St. Nistheros the Great, one of the desert fathers, was asked, "What good work should I be doing?" He responded, "Do whatever your soul desires according to God, and guard your heart." Yes, we keep the commandments and remain faithful to the Church, that is, "according to God," and then we are free to listen to the guidance within our heart.

The human heart as found in Scripture, particularly in the Psalms, is very interesting. The heart meditates, desires, is vexed, has secrets, is deep, can be smitten, withers like grass, or melts like wax. It pants like a deer for streams of water. It cries out to God and can be broken, contrite, and made clean. The heart is the center of the human person, the source of everything we are. Obviously, in the Bible the heart has a life of its own, a *healing* life of its own.

The human heart is the entrance to an inner chapel where we can hear, with all creation, praise to God. The heart is the entrance to love, to the place of healing balm. The love of God, a matter of the heart, heals all.

Healing restores peace. In *Unseen Warfare* we read,

> *Peace of heart is both the aim of spiritual warfare and the most powerful means to achieve victory in it. When passionate turmoil steals into the heart [and doesn't this happen to us all the time], do not jump to attack the passion in an effort to overcome it, but descend into your heart [physical, then spiritual] and strive to restore quiet there.*[15]

We go into our heart and stay until we are calm. The guideline is clear. It is simple, yet hard to do.

I once visited the Monastery of the Holy Dormition in

---

15 Nicodemus, *Unseen Warfare*, p. 257.

Rives Junction, Michigan. Father Roman Braga, the founding father of the monastery, was there, vibrant as ever. During the few moments I had with him alone, he said that when he was in the Romanian concentration camp, the officials tried to destroy the intellectuals by putting them in solitary confinement without their books. The theory was that this would break the intellectuals' spirit because it would remove their stimulation and their connection with each other.

> *We have within our heart an inner space more expansive than outer space.*

Father Roman said that for him, there was "no place to go." He didn't have anything outside himself for solace. He then made a startling statement: "So I went into my inner universe." When I heard that, time stood still for me. I knew I was in the presence of mystery, in the presence of a man who had been somewhere I had never been. It was as if he said, "Let me tell you what it felt like to put my foot on the moon." I have never put my foot on the moon and have no idea what the experience would be like. Father Roman's "inner universe" is a place for all of us to ponder, to seek, to hope to enter.

Our home is where the heart is and where we find welcome. According to *The Art of Prayer,*

Your own home is paradise after an absence. Exactly the same feeling comes when, after distraction, we return to attention and to the inner life. When we are in the heart, we are at home; when we are not in the heart, we are homeless. And it is about this above all that we must take trouble.[16]

We are on a journey through the inward space of the *heart*, a journey that is not measured by the movement of the clock, for it is a journey out of time into eternity. We have within our heart an "inner space" that is more expansive than outer space, more vast than the cosmos.

The outer limits of the human person are extremely wide; each of us knows very little about his or her true and deep self. "Within the *heart* are unfathomable depths," St. Macarius affirms in his *Homilies*. "It is but a *small vessel* and yet dragons and lions are there, and there poisonous creatures and all the treasures of wickedness; rough, uneven paths are there, and gaping chasms. There likewise is God, there are the angels, there life and the Kingdom, there light and the Apostles, the heavenly cities and the treasures of grace; all things are there."

The Physical Heart

As st. theophan said, the heart is something existing on the material level, a part of our body, the center of our organism

---

16 Chariton of Valamo, comp., *The Art of Prayer* (London: Faber & Faber, 1977), p. 192.

from the physical point of view. This material aspect of the heart must not be overlooked. When Orthodox ascetical texts speak of the heart, they mean (among other things) the "carnal heart," a piece of muscular flesh, which is not to be understood solely in a symbolic or metaphorical sense.

St. Gregory Palamas said, "Can you not see how essential it is that those who have determined to pay attention to themselves in inner quiet should gather together in mind and enclose it in the body, and especially in that 'body,' which we call the heart."[17]

The heart weighs almost a pound and is about the size of an adult's fist. For such a small organ, it does Herculean work, beating about one hundred thousand times a day. Unlike raising our arm, we don't "beat" our heart. Rather, the human heart is autonomic—that is, it beats of its own accord. Better said, God beats our heart, keeps it beating one hundred thousand times a day.[18]

Fascinatingly, the saints speak of the heart as the locus of God, and they mean that we begin with an awareness of the physical heart to then move into the awareness of the spiritual heart. Metropolitan Kallistos Ware says in the introduction to *The Art of Prayer*, "Observe that prayer of the *heart* is not only prayer of the soul and spirit but also of the *body*. It must

17   G. E. H. Palmer, Philip Sherrard, and Kallistos Ware, *The Philokalia: The Complete Text*, vol. 4 (London: Faber & Faber, 1995), p. 334.

18   A highly technical but informative book on the heart and brain is Mark Bear and Barry Connors, *Neuroscience: Exploring the Brain* (Baltimore, MD: Lippincott, Williams and Wilkins, 2007).

not be forgotten that the heart signifies, among other things, a bodily organ. The body has a positive role to play in the work of prayer."[19]

St. Ignatius Brianchaninov said, "When we read in the Fathers about the place of the heart which the mind finds by prayer, we must understand by this the spiritual faculty that exists in the heart. Placed by the Creator in the upper part of the heart, this spiritual faculty distinguishes the human heart from the heart of animals. . . . The spiritual faculty in the heart manifests itself—independently of the intellect."

Into the *heart*, then, a person descends—into his natural heart, and from there into the "deep" heart—into that "inner closet" which is no longer of the flesh. The human heart is much more than a mechanical pump. Until recently the heart was seen as a passive relay station. Research in the 1960s and 1970s discovered that the physical heart is an organ of great intelligence with its own nervous system, decision-making powers, and connections to the brain. The research found that the heart actually "talks" with the brain. The heart has its own logic.

In the 1990s, cardiologists introduced a new concept, the "heart brain." Each beat of the heart sends complex signals to the brain and other organs. The heart not only has a language of its own but its own mind. The awareness of heart intelligence is sometimes called intuition.

The heart is exquisitely sensitive to emotions and emits an

---

19   Chariton, *The Art of Prayer*, p. 22.

energy field five thousand times stronger than the brain's, one that can be measured more than ten feet away.

The physical heart is where we place our awareness to enter into the realm of the spiritual heart. But hearing our heartbeat is a delicate challenge. Once I was walking with my wife during a winter snowfall. It was early evening. We'd had dinner, the children were safe, and we decided to walk outside to be in the snow-scene together. She stopped and said, "Al, listen to the snow falling."

I was stunned. I could see the snowflakes against the street-light. But I had no idea falling snow was audible. I began to be quiet and simply listen. Sure enough, the beautiful, soft sounds of snow falling were available for me, once I had "ears to hear." Throughout her lifetime, my wife taught me to tune my ears to sounds of beauty. The beating of a human heart is rather like the sound of snow falling. It is audible to those with ears to hear.

A statement attributed to Sartre said that if God's voice is present for human hearts, the sound of His voice would be like the "flutter of a bird's wing." Thoughtful imagery. I can hardly hear the sound of a semi lumbering down the street, let alone hear the flutter of a bird's wing. We all have much quieting down to do to become aware of our physical heartbeat.

> *The Jesus Prayer is called the prayer of the heart.*

Descending into the Heart

OUR TASK IN PRAYER is to unite the intellect and the heart, to find the place of the heart and draw the intellect down into it. There, when the heart has been found and the intellect is devoted to guarding it, true prayer, the prayer of the heart, becomes possible. The Jesus Prayer is called the prayer of the heart.

> *Where is the heart? Where sadness, joy, anger, and other emotions are felt, here is the heart. Stand there with attention. The physical heart is a piece of muscular flesh, but it is not the flesh that feels, but the soul; the carnal heart serves as an instrument for these feelings, just as the brain serves as an instrument for the mind. Stand in the heart, with the faith that God is also there, but how He is there do not speculate. . . . The heart is to be understood here, not in its ordinary meaning, but in the sense of "inner man." We have within us an inner man, or a hidden man of the heart. It is the God-like spirit that was breathed into the first man, and it remains with us continuously, even after the Fall. . . . It shows itself in the certainty of God's existence.*

These are the teachings of St. Theophan in *The Art of Prayer*.

How can we learn to stop talking and to start listening? Instead of simply speaking to God, how can we make our own the prayer in which God speaks to us? One way to begin this journey *inward* is through the invocation of the Name. We can repeat "Lord Jesus," according to Metropolitan Kallistos Ware.[20]

---

20 Kallistos Ware, *The Power of the Name* (Fairacres, Oxford: SLG Press, 1986), p. 3.

It is not a matter of getting the mind to have no thoughts. St. Diadochos of Photike noted that there is a dimension of the mind that is always doing something. So we give it something to do by repeating a short phrase gently and regularly. He tells us we can give our intellect nothing but the prayer "Lord Jesus." We concentrate on these words within our inner shrine. "Lord Jesus."

St. Theophan said, "Do not be lazy about descending into the heart. In the heart is life, and you must live there. Do not think it is something to be attempted only by the perfect. No. It is for everyone who has begun to seek the Lord."

Father Lev Gillet is very explicit that the name of Jesus alone can be the "prayer word" for some seeking Christians. He said,

> The invocation of the Name of Jesus can be put into many frames. It is for each person to find the form, the frame, which is the most appropriate to his or her own prayer. But, whatever formula may be used, the heart and center of the invocation must be the Holy Name itself, the word Jesus. There resides the whole strength of the invocation. The Name of Jesus may either be used alone or be inserted in a more or less developed phrase. In the East the commonest form is: "Lord Jesus Christ, Son of God, have mercy on me a sinner." One might simply say: "Jesus Christ" or "Lord Jesus." The invocation may be reduced to one single word, "Jesus." This last form—the Name of Jesus only—is the most ancient mould of the invocation of the Name. It is the shortest, the simplest and, as we think, the easiest. Therefore, without deprecating the other formulas, we suggest that the word "Jesus" alone should be used. Thus, when we speak of the invocation of the Name, we meant the devout and frequent repetition

*of the Name itself, of the word 'Jesus' without additions. The
holy Name is the prayer. The Name of Jesus may be pronounced
or silently thought.*[21]

Father Lev Gillet recommends the single word, *Jesus*, as the
"prayer word" for some people to simplify and focus attention.

Johnny Appleseed

WHEN WE DESCEND into our heart, we discover who we are
and where we are going. One fine example of a person who lived
out of his heart is the American folk hero Johnny Appleseed.

Legend and fact blend into a mixture of pleasant folklore,
but a few things are certain. Johnny Appleseed was a real person named John Chapman who lived in the nineteenth century.
Another fact is that the US Post Office made a commemorative
stamp of Johnny Appleseed, complete with first-day issue and
usable postage stamps.[22]

I must admit that Johnny Appleseed is a folk hero of mine.
The part of his tale that smites me is that he rarely retraced his
steps. Generally, he walked one way, westward, without looking
back much. He planted seeds and kept on walking. He lived as a
celibate, was called a missionary by some, and died and is buried
in Fort Wayne, Indiana.

---

21 Lev Gillet, *On the Invocation of the Name of Jesus* (Springfield, IL: Templegate Publishers, 1985), p. 14.

22 There is much material on the Internet about Johnny Appleseed.

The question of how such a man could attain such status in the American imagination haunted me. He didn't lead armies into victorious battles, nor did he found settlements or govern colonies. All he did was plant apple seeds. Like many in ministry today, Johnny Appleseed planted seeds and didn't see much of the fruit of his labor. Apple trees don't grow overnight.

He carried a leather sack filled with apple seeds that he acquired free at cider mills. He planted apple trees as he moved westward from Pennsylvania through the Ohio Valley, and later into Indiana and other states. He was rather odd, wearing old clothes and not staying long in any one place. He was known to give his better clothing to people he felt needed it more than he.

His dream was to produce so many apples that no one would ever go hungry. It was a rather lofty, one might say biblical, dream. He was also very religious and preached to people along the way. His favorite book was his Bible. He made friends with Indian tribes and was known to have learned many Indian languages well enough to converse. He lived on food provided by nature, and he never killed animals.

One summer, as my vacation, I decided to drive on a quest to discover more about Johnny Appleseed. My pilgrimage was fully rewarded. I discovered many city and country parks named after him. And I found a city in the Midwest that puts on an annual play recounting his life and deeds. I talked with people who hold him in the highest regard.

At the end of my venture, my question about his importance

was answered. I visited his tombstone in a large campground in Fort Wayne, Indiana, complete with baseball diamonds, swimming pools, and family campers. Interestingly, he is not buried in a cemetery. Rather, his is the only grave in the park, located on a small mound surrounded by neatly cut shrubbery.

The answer to my question came as I gazed at the small plaque atop his burial stone. The plaque, like his life, was simple and clear. It said, "He lived for others." The American imagination and the US Post Office commemorate a human being who lived a life of self-giving. No doubt, Johnny Appleseed was, and is, a healing presence to many, giving them strength and hope.

> *"He lived for others."*

Along with my own personal saints, Johnny Appleseed ranks high as a model for me to emulate. I need to learn to plant seeds as best I can and not look for appreciation or results. The value comes in the planting—and in becoming aware that it is Christ who is the planter, working in me to plant the seeds to spread His Word. More important, perhaps, is an awareness that He gives the fruit as and when He wills.

The Voice of God in the Heart

AWARENESS OF OUR BREATHING opens a door to awareness of the presence of God, the giver of breath, and it is the very voice of God, guiding and encouraging us. No one has power to command the heart. It lives its own special life. It rejoices of itself, it is sad of itself; and no one can do anything about this. Only the Master of all has power to enter the heart, to put feelings into it independently of its naturally changing currents.

St. Theophan compared the heart to a lever. The lever that controls all our activities is the heart. Here are formed the convictions and sympathies that determine the will and give it strength.

The story is told of the third-grade boy who went to the school nurse for a routine health check. The nurse put the stethoscope on his chest and recorded his heart rate. She then asked, "Have you ever heard your own heart beating?"

He replied, "No, ma'am." She put the stethoscope on his chest with the earbuds in his ears. The boy heard the lub-dub, lub-dub of his heart beating. Sheepishly, he asked, "Is that Jesus knocking?"

Someone had taught that boy the meaning of Revelation 3:20: "Behold, I stand at the door and knock. If anyone hears My voice and opens the door, I will come in to him and dine with him, and he with Me." Indeed, the Lord does stand at the door of our heart, moment by moment, and knocks, hoping we will hear His voice and open the door so He can come in and dine with us—that is, have communion with us throughout the day and night.

Within the heart is the antenna for the voice of God. We

keep our heart open and pure as much as we can, to keep the antenna receptive. St. Isaac the Syrian said that "it is better to acquire purity of heart than to convert whole nations of heathens from error."[23]

> *St. Isaac the Syrian said, "It is better to acquire purity of heart than to convert whole nations of heathens from error."*

---

23 Ware, *Inner Kingdom*, p. 110, quoting St. Isaac the Syrian, *Homily* 4.

CHAPTER 4

Vocation as a Way of Life

MY VOCATION IS NOT MY CAREER or my role in life. Rather, my vocation is my call from Christ to do what He has me on the planet to do, to cooperate in building up His Kingdom on earth. Hence, my vocation is fluid and changes with each passing day, each passing moment, in an enthralling adventure. My vocation is my way of life—His way of life in me—as time passes.

Every person has the same vocation. Every person is created in the image and likeness of God and has the vocation to live out that image and likeness. Each is called to "be perfect, just as your Father in heaven is perfect" (Matt. 5:48).

Every person also has a different vocation. God has an inimitable, exclusive vocation for every person. Within each singular vocation, each person is called in a different way to love God fully and her neighbor as herself, uniquely.

> *Healing takes place in a spiritual realm where God provides the balm of restoration.*

Ann Bezzerides, director of the Office of Vocation Ministry at Hellenic College, tells us, "When we live life as vocation, we witness to the world of the kingdom of God and rejoice in that gift that gives ultimate meaning to our daily, complex lives."[24]

For our purposes, every person is called to be a healing presence—that is, to love others. Each person, even the hermit or terminally ill person in a nursing home, is called to be a healing presence. Becoming a healing presence for others extends beyond geography and boundaries. Healing takes place in a spiritual realm where God provides the balm of restoration.

Christ provides everything in our quest to be a healing presence. He provides the opportunity for us to have encounters with others, the heart-awareness to know what to say and do, another person to be a healing presence for, and the life-energy to actually make a difference with another person.

As inscribed on the icon of Christ in the Chapel of St. Vladimir's Seminary, "You have not chosen Me. I have chosen you"

---

24 Ann Mitsakos Bezzerides, ed., *Christ at Work: Orthodox Christian Perspectives on Vocation* (Brookline, MA: Holy Cross Orthodox Press, 2006), p. 11.

(John 15:16). God knows what He is doing in choosing me to do His particular, unique set of tasks today, unequipped as I seem to be. As one saying has it, "God does not call the equipped. He equips the called."

In my own case, my conversion to Orthodoxy over thirty years ago is one of the best things ever to happen to me. I did not convert as the result of a systematic search for Truth. I did not convert because I read extensively and concluded that Orthodoxy was the "right" religion. No. I was married, and my wife was Orthodox, so we went to the Orthodox Divine Liturgy every other week. I had become a Quaker after forty years in another Christian religion. As a family we went to a Quaker service one week and the Orthodox Divine Liturgy the next week. It seemed to work for everyone. I suppose I could have been content with that strange arrangement for the long run. However, God had other plans, as I now see.

One Sunday I woke with the clear idea that I wanted to convert to Orthodoxy. Simple and clear. When my wife awoke, I told her. She said, "Al, please don't convert for me or you'll resent me for it for the rest of your life." I said I would not do that to her. But I also said I didn't have an Orthodox voice or Orthodox legs. I can't sing a note, and I can't stand for long services. In a sense, I backed into Orthodoxy. I was not equipped to become Orthodox in the usual sense of the word. God chose me to become Orthodox, as I was and am, and I am eternally grateful. That's all I know.

Our vocation pivots on being called and on accepting the call of God.

Of course, fulfilling our vocation depends on synergy. We must cooperate with grace. We do our part through acceptance and stillness. We then become a conduit of fire—the fire of the Godhead, hotter than the sun. The fire of God comes into us, goes through us, and moves out to another person. We simply allow the fire to go through us. But it is a healing fire nonetheless. Of course, the conduit is empty and hollow, and Christ could put it aside at any time. But He often chooses to use the conduit to heal others by His power flowing through it.

My task is to find gratitude in all circumstances, including negative life situations. We also need to know the cost. A college student said to me, "If I decide to put Christ first, the suffering will be great but the joy will be greater." Many of us shrink from becoming a healing presence to others because of the initial cost. We don't experience the full joy because we get stuck in the suffering. Joy emerges by living *through* the suffering to the other side.

We can look at that same insight by turning the telescope around. If I put all things in God's hands, I will see God's hands in all things. That's my vocation, to see God's hands in all that I do and say.

A Modern Good Samaritan

As I begin to live out my unique vocation as a healing presence, I begin to see myself differently. My self-image changes. I begin to see myself for who I really am, "the light of the world" (Matt. 5:14). As my self-image changes, I begin to act slightly differently. I begin to be more aware of the real needs of others as they present themselves before me as needs for strength and hope—that is, healing. I also begin to be more aware of when others, consciously or unconsciously, provide me with strength and hope; hence they are also a healing presence for me.

A friend of mine, a forty-year-old man with severe obsessive-compulsive disorder, can't seem to do much of anything productive. I'll call him Jonathan. He spends much time in inner blackness, often crying for hours on end. He successfully battles suicidal inclinations that haunt him on occasion. He walks his dog, reads books, and occasionally goes to a church service. His weekdays and weekends are extraordinarily lonely. He sometimes dips into gambling and Internet pornography.

Jonathan sees himself as having not much to give to others, as a sponge that sucks in and gives little out. His self-image is very low. I can also say that God is slowly changing this for him. He has gotten a job and is relating much better to others.

One evening Jonathan had a free coupon to gamble a small amount of money at the local casino. He decided not to bring a credit card or money, but merely to go to the casino and gamble the coupon money away. While driving to the casino, he passed a disabled car with a young man standing on the side of the road. In a blink (read, intuition from the Lord), Jonathan did a U-turn and stopped to see if he could help.

The young man didn't have the suitable tools to change his flat tire. So Jonathan drove him to the nearby small town, where they bought the tools. They drove back to the disabled car. The new tools didn't fit the bolts on the car. The only solution was to drive the other way, a longer distance, and buy a new tire. Jonathan said he was peaceful about not doing his own will by going to the casino, and he drove the young man to buy a new tire. They returned and put the new tire on the car. The problem was solved, and the grateful young man drove into the night. The entire episode lasted a few hours.

Jonathan said that during the saga, he and the man talked about life's circumstances. Jonathan has a small chrome fish, a symbol of Christ, on the back of his car. The young man asked Jonathan if he was Christian. Jonathan said yes and humbly added that he wasn't a very good one. Among other things, Jonathan does not attend church regularly. The young man said that he, too, was a "not very good" Christian. Then they talked about something else.

No doubt, the young man knew he had met a human who, in his moment of need, delivered help. In effect, Jonathan was a living Christian, a good Samaritan, to the young man in his moment of need. No doubt, Jonathan lived out his vocation of becoming a healing presence that evening as he was called by the Lord.

Naming Others as a Vocation

OUR VOCATION IS TO HEAL others into Christ. When we meet others in our environment or in our head, we can bring healing ointment by bringing Christ.

We heal others by saying the Name of Jesus over them. Father Lev Gillet said, "The Name of Jesus is a concrete and powerful means of transfiguring persons into their hidden, innermost, utmost reality." Isn't that what others are looking for from us, especially youth? Don't they want us to see and communicate, sometimes without words, the goodness in them that they can't see themselves?

Metropolitan Anthony of Sourozh has a profound insight to offer us:

> *Unless we look at a person and see the beauty there is in this person, we can contribute nothing to him. One does not help a person by discerning what is wrong, what is ugly, what is distorted. Christ looked at everyone he met, at the prostitute, at the thief, and saw the beauty hidden there. Perhaps it was distorted, perhaps damaged, but it was beauty none the less, and what he did was to call out this beauty.*[25]

---

25 From a homily preached on August 14, 1983.

Father Lev Gillet said,

> *We should approach all men and women—in the street, the shop, the office, the factory, the bus, the queue, and especially those who seem irritating and antagonistic—with the Name of Jesus in our heart and on our lips. We should pronounce His Name over them all, for their real Name is the Name of Jesus.*[26]

Our attitude is extended love for them as we name them with His Name in a spirit of adoration, dedication, and service. Fr. Gillet admonishes us to adore Christ in them, serve Christ in them. In many of these men and women—in the malicious, in the criminal—Jesus is imprisoned. Deliver Him in them.

One semester, St. Vladimir's seminarians did their field-work at the local prison. The seminarians became aware that the prisoners were rarely treated as humans and that when they are respected first, they respond with dignity and appreciation. The seminarians did weekly Bible studies and some counseling with the prisoners.

One week the weather kept the seminarians from going to the prison. The next week the prisoners expressed disappointment and said they missed the routine visits of the seminarians. Yes, the prisoners have a hard life. Yes, the prisoners are humans with soft hearts, as created by our Lord, and they are grateful for anyone who would come into the prison as a healing presence.

As we name others with the name of Jesus, our vision

---

26 Lev Gillet, *On the Invocation of the Name of Jesus* (Springfield, IL: Templegate Publishers, 1985), p. 57.

changes. If we go through the world with this new vision, saying "Jesus" over every person, seeing Jesus in every person, everybody will be transformed and transfigured before our eyes. The more we are ready to give of ourselves to others, the more will our new vision be clear and vivid. Rightly did Jacob say to Esau, when they were reconciled, "No, please, if I have now found favor in your sight, then receive my present from my hand, inasmuch as I have seen your face as though I had seen the face of God" (Gen. 33:10). Christ changes us as we allow Him to change others through us.

Subtraction as Growth

SANCTITY AND SANITY are the same reality, as revealed in the Person of Jesus. He is sanctity, or holiness, personified. He is sanity, or emotional and cognitive stability, personified. The question for us is, "How can we become more saintly and more sane as we live our vocation?" For starters, the process is one of elimination, of ridding ourselves of the darkness clouding the Light.

> *Sanctity is a process of subtraction.*

Sanctity is a process of subtraction, not addition or multiplication or division. We subtract our resistances to grace. Christ subtracts the defenses we build against His power in us.

Like the peeling of an onion, we allow Christ to peel away (read, subtract) the layers of our outer shell to reveal our light within, His healing presence within us.

We never know when "suddenly" is coming our way. I met my wife through a process of subtraction. Long story short, at the time I met her, I was interested in another woman. I asked that woman out for dinner on a Saturday evening. She said she had been waiting for me to ask her, but she already had plans for dinner. She asked me to please call her the following week. I was thrilled that she was willing to go out with me but disappointed that I had nothing to do that Saturday evening.

Only then did I realize I had an invitation to a wedding where I knew no one except the bride and groom. The sequence here is important. My will and God's will. I wanted one woman, and God had other plans. Frankly, I didn't want to go to the wedding. I proceeded to have an internal argument: my desire not to go to the wedding versus the wedding invitation. The wedding invitation won.

When I arrived at the Roman Catholic Church early, as is my custom, I sat in the middle of a row in the middle of the church. There was no one within ten feet of me in any direction. I felt isolated, lonely, and distraught. Then a gorgeous young woman with a guitar came out to practice a few songs with us. By that time other people had arrived. I immediately noticed that the guitarist wasn't wearing an engagement or wedding ring, so I decided to try to dance with her during the reception.

Her voice was heavenly, and her personality turned out to be enchanting. We danced. I got her phone number, took her out the next week, and married her two years later. By the way, I did date the other woman and quickly discovered that she was a fine person but there was no chemistry between us. The point of this little anecdote is clear. I wanted to spend that Saturday evening with one woman, and the Lord wanted me to spend it with the woman who would become my wife.

I had to subtract—or actually allow the Lord to subtract—my previous expectations and all my hesitations. I had to let go and live. As it turns out, all the good I have in my life now came to me through that lovely woman who became my wife. When we met, I was a tenured guidance counselor in a large public high school. After we became engaged, she said to me, "Al, you're too bright to be a guidance counselor. Quit and get a doctorate in psychology. I'm a nurse. I'll work, and we'll do fine."

I looked at her as if she were crazy. I liked my job. I had tenure. Most of the teachers envied my position; I didn't have to prepare classes, give and grade exams, face twenty-five students at a time all day long. And I got paid more. But, as she suggested, I quit. I took a year to prepare for application into a doctoral program and did eventually get a doctorate in psychology.

More than that, I was a lapsed Roman Catholic when I met my wife. Through her I converted to Orthodoxy. Now I teach at St. Vladimir's Seminary and have many fine friends in Orthodoxy that I would not have met otherwise. Through my wife I have two adult children and three grandchildren. It is no exaggeration to say that all the good I have in my life came from the Lord through my wife. And we could never have met except at that wedding. The Lord subtracted my agenda on that auspicious day in May and gave me a lifetime, an eternity really, of unbounded gifts. I now have an eternal marriage.

Subtraction Leads to Joy

OUR UNIQUE VOCATION IS TO LIVE, moment by moment, the way Christ wants us to live. He is the Way. He came to show us the way. And He told us how to find the way. He said, "These things I have spoken to you, that My joy may remain in you, and *that* your joy may be full" (John 15:11). Clearly Jesus wants us to have joy and to spread joy. When we spread joy, we give others strength and hope, thereby becoming a healing presence.

In his book *For the Life of the World*, Father Alexander Schmemann, a man who exuded joy, spoke glowingly of the place of joy in the Christian life. He said that the "great joy" is the context from which everything else in Christianity developed and acquired its meaning. "'For behold,' the angel said to the shepherds, 'I bring you good tiding of great joy.' Thus begins the Gospel, and its end is, 'And they worshipped Him and returned to Jerusalem with great joy' (Luke 2:10; 24:52). And we must recover the meaning of this great joy."[27]

Father Schmemann reminds us, "From the very beginning Christianity has been the proclamation of joy, of the only possible joy on earth. . . . Of all accusations against Christians, the most terrible one was uttered by Nietzsche when he said that Christians have no joy."

> *Of all accusations against Christians, the most terrible one was uttered by Nietzsche when he said that Christians have no joy.*

In a series of quotations, Father Schmemann said the following:

> *If there is something that we—the serious, adult and frustrated Christians of the twentieth century—look at with suspicion, it is certainly joy. . . . The modern world has relegated joy to the category of "fun" and "relaxation."*

> *We are called to live in the world seeing everything in it as a revelation of God, a sign of His presence, the joy of His coming.*

> *Christian mission [vocation] is always at its beginning. It is today that I am sent back into the world in joy and peace. Joy, however, is not something one can define or analyze. One enters into joy. "Enter thou into the joy of thy Lord" (Matt. 25:21).*

---

27   Alexander Schmemann, *For the Life of the World* (Crestwood, NY: St. Vladimir's Seminary Press, 1973), p. 24.

. . . We enter through the source and the fulfillment of joy, the very sacrament of joy, the Eucharist.[28]

In his Epistle, St. James challenges his readers regarding joy: "My brethren, count it all joy when you fall into various trials" (James 1:2). Joy amid trials is counterintuitive. Our first reaction to trials of any sort is to shrink and decry the situation. Our gut reaction is to avoid trials. Jesus experienced our inclination when in the Garden He said, "O My Father, if it is possible, let this cup pass from Me" (Matt. 26:39). Going beyond our initial reaction, we say with Jesus, "Nevertheless, not as I will, but as You *will*." And therein we can count it all joy as St. James suggests.

Our vocation is to be real witnesses to the joy and peace of the Holy Spirit, to that new life of which we are made partakers in the Church.

> *A Christian is one who, wherever he looks, finds Christ and rejoices in Him.*

St. Hesychius of Jerusalem has some words we can apply to joy. He said, "Great care should be taken to preserve that which is precious. But for us only one thing is truly precious . . . the invocation of Jesus Christ." It is no coincidence that the word *invocation* has, for us in this chapter, a special connotation of "in-vocation," or "in my vocation."

---

28 Schmemann, *Life of the World*, p. 25.

We can apply the words of St. Hesychius to preserving that joy in our heart, that joy [read, pearl of great price] that Christ said He came to bring us.[29]

An Orthodox icon shows light as coming from within the person depicted. Similarly, we can have joy come from within us. We can be suffused with joy by God's grace. To *suffuse* means to spread over or through something, to fill, to saturate, to permeate, to imbue. We saturate the space we occupy with the light of joy.

Father Schmemann said, "A Christian is one who, wherever he looks, finds Christ and rejoices in Him. This joy transforms all his human plans and projects, decisions and actions, making all his mission [vocation] the sacrament of the world's return to Him who is the life of the world."

Blossom Where You Are Planted

ABBA ANTHONY TOLD Abba Poemen that the great temptation is to fail to be what God wants us to be. He added that a man is "always to take blame for his own sins and expect temptation to the last breath."[30]

One great temptation in life is to imagine something better

---

29 E. Kadloubovsky and G. E. H. Palmer, *Writings from the Philokalia on Prayer of the Heart* (London: Faber & Faber, 1961), p. 99.

30 Benedicta Ward, trans., *The Sayings of the Desert Fathers* (Kalamazoo, MI: Cistercian Publications, 1975), p. 2.

somewhere else, over the imagined rainbow. We can't keep imagined thoughts from entering our mind, but we can use those thoughts to pray.

St. Hesychius of Jerusalem tells us, as it is impossible to cross the expanse of the sea without a large ship, so without calling on Jesus Christ it is impossible to banish from the soul the suggestion of a wicked thought.

> *Everyone should remain in the state in which he was called.*

We remain in the Church to stabilize us. The Church exists to preserve our sanity.

St. Paul exhorts us, "Let each one remain in the same calling in which he was called" (1 Cor. 7:20). We don't become rootless. We stay where we are planted unless God, through the approval of our spiritual father, clearly wants us to move on.

CHAPTER 5

Gentleness
as a Mindset

....

WE BEGIN WHERE WE ALWAYS BEGIN, with the words of Christ. "Take My yoke upon you, and learn from Me; for I am gentle and lowly in heart, and you will find rest for your souls" (Matt. 11:29). And we continue with a quote from St. Seraphim of Sarov:

> You cannot be too gentle, too kind. Avoid even appearing harsh in your treatment of each other. Joy, radiant joy, streams from the face of him who gives and kindles joy in the heart of him who receives. All condemnation is from the devil. Never condemn each other. We condemn others only because we avoid knowing ourselves. When we gaze at our own failings, we see such a swamp that nothing in another can equal it. That is why we turn away, and make much of the faults of others. Instead of condemning others, strive to reach inner peace. Keep silent, refrain from judgment. This will raise you above the deadly arrows

of slander, insult and outrage and will shield your glowing hearts against all evil.[31]

Gentleness as a mindset seems to be emblematic of St. Seraphim; it is apparent in his writings and his posture in icons. He gives us a living portrait of a man who was a healing presence to humans—and, it is said, even to a bear.

Being gentle does not exclude being firm.

Being gentle does not exclude being firm. Jesus was firm. Mother Teresa was known for her gentleness, but there are many anecdotes about her that demonstrate her firmness. A story is told of a visit by Mother Teresa to New York City to give a talk at the United Nations. She was being driven on the FDR Highway along the East River, where traffic speeds along with no pull-off lane on the right, only a concrete wall. A tire on the car suddenly blew out. The driver pulled the car into the right lane and put on the flashing lights.

Mother Teresa said to the driver, "Let's leave the car. Get out and hail a ride." The driver, a priest, said, "Mother, this is New York City." So she firmly and gently got out of the car, hailed a passing car, and was driven to the United Nations, leaving the priest and the car. Granted it was Mother Teresa, and a passerby would recognize her in white and blue. Still, she was

---

31 Judy Zimmerman Herr and Robert Herr, *Transforming Violence: Linking Local and Global Peacemaking* (Scottsdale, PA: Herald Press, 1998), p. 32.

undaunted in her gentle but firm resolve to do what she was called to do.

When we are authentically gentle, we are simultaneously bold and courageous. Gentleness is not associated with being a doormat.

From the writings of the desert fathers we have an exquisite example of gentleness from the anecdote told about Abba Poemen: "An old man asked Abba Poemen if he saw a brother nodding in church whether he should nudge him to wake him up for the vigil. Abba Poemen answered, 'Now, if I see a brother nodding I lay his head on my knees and give him rest.'"[32] That's a vivid example of one desert father's gentleness toward other human beings.

Aging as Growth in Gentleness

WHEN I CONVERTED TO ORTHODOXY, the priest who was instructing me in the faith told me that after death, the memory or image we have of the dead person is like an icon. That is to say, the bad qualities of the dead person fall away and the good qualities emerge, rather like figure and background. As time passes, there is more figure in front, good qualities, and the background, bad qualities, diminishes.

---

32 Derwas J. Chitty, *The Desert a City* (Crestwood, NY: SVS Press, 1995, p. 71.

As I've watched people grow old, I've noticed that generally the people I know and love become gentler with the passing years. For example, my mother died at 102. She was an admirable Italian woman, whom I often refer to as a Pasta Mamma. She had a feisty side to her, though it didn't come out too much. As life went on, I noticed the feisty side reduce until it virtually evaporated into the atmosphere. That has happened with many people I know; a slow life transformation occurs toward gentleness. It is also true that not all aging people become gentler. Someone said that as we grow old, we either become charmingly childlike or boringly infantile.

A man is happy so long as he chooses to be happy, and nothing can stop him, according to Solzhenitsyn.

I know a small group of living people whom I consider extraordinary and who are becoming perceptibly gentler. That small group includes a few seminarians and others who might be considered as unlikely candidates, too young or too hardhearted. However, I know them well enough to know their life struggle, and I admire them very much. Perhaps it is their gentleness that attracts me to them. But it is not only the gentleness; there is also a certain kind of heroism of choice, a commitment to the Christian lifestyle. Maybe the two go together.

Gentleness is closely aligned with tenderness, a careful, strong, yet very soft touch. I think of the fingers of Jesus on icons. Jesus' fingers are gentle, beckoning, inviting, and signifying the power within His humanity. In the Bible are recorded many times when Jesus used His fingers very tenderly to touch the ears or the mouth of someone in need of healing. Jesus had no fear of gently touching other humans in an appropriate way. He used His fingers to write carefully in the sand to help a needy woman. So Jesus is our model of extreme humility and of extreme gentleness.

> *Gentleness is closely aligned with tenderness, a careful, strong, yet very soft touch.*

For our purposes, apart from Jesus, there is no greater person to show us the model of true gentleness than the Theotokos. In her icons, the Theotokos shows us clearly a model of firm gentleness, especially the icons that show her holding the infant Jesus.

As a clinical psychologist, I often find myself saying to a counselee, "Please be gentle with yourself." Most of my job, of course, is listening. I am often struck by how often counselees set themselves up for failure as they speak about a personal rule of discipline. Often their resolutions are over the top—that is, very difficult to carry out in any sustained way. Often counselees need help to factor in the possibility that they won't be able to carry out their plans every day or every week.

Many of us don't have an image of ourselves like the image God has of us. We don't have a strong sense of loving gentleness toward ourselves. Hence, we get into a performance mentality, a mindset that tightens our brow, flexes our mental muscle, and tries to do too much, not because God is calling us to do so much, but because pride and ego want to perform better. Yes, we can be gentle with ourselves within an ascetical life of integrity.

Gentleness through a Soft Smile

WE CAN TAKE TO HEART these words of Mother Teresa: "Love Jesus and keep a smiling heart for Him." We might ask, what is a smiling heart? Of course, a smiling heart is a matter of attitude, an inner light of delight. A smiling heart expresses itself in a soft smile, especially when alone. When we are alone, we are never really alone. Jesus is always present, whether we are cognizant of it or not. When we are aware of His abiding presence, how can we not have a soft smile of appreciation and joy?

Mother Teresa also said, "Accept all He gives and whatever He takes with a big smile. For this is holiness—to do His will with a big smile." The Lord wants us to joyfully desire His way, His plans, His will.

Smiling can be a special challenge when things get rough. By faith, we know that Christ is not apart from us during times of trial and sorrow. Metropolitan Anthony Bloom said, "The greater the opposition, the greater also is the evidence that help is at hand. The devil never attacks us so violently as when we are quite close to the end of our strength."[33] Hence, the greater the inner or outer opposition, the greater the call for a soft smile.

You might ask, how can I become more of a healing presence? Sometimes we are looking for influential deeds or striking interventions. Mother Teresa said, "I will never understand all the good a simple smile can accomplish." Perhaps a good concrete way to begin to become a healing presence is to smile softly more, even when alone.

Gentleness Respects Boundaries

METROPOLITAN TIKHON of the Orthodox Church in America told this anecdote at his election. As a young monk he went to Mount Athos. While he was there, he encountered an old monk carrying a bag. The young monk, Tikhon, offered to carry the old man's bag. The old man refused, saying, "No, I need to carry my own bag." Metropolitan Tikhon said he learned a valuable lesson that day. He learned that he must carry his own bag. He also learned that he must allow others to carry their own bag. So, as a healing presence, we need to be present for others and allow them to carry their own bag and deal with their own issues, without trying to save them from their pain or control the outcome of their plight.

---

33 Anthony Bloom, *Living Prayer* (Springfield, IL: Templegate Publishers, 1996), p. 48.

I need to know where my boundaries are and to allow others to know my limitations. Many in the helping professions and in the clergy suffer from a savior complex. This complex, also called a martyr complex or messiah complex, is based on the notion that I am, or am destined to be, the savior of others by my own power. Of course, this attitude can be lethal to the healing and well-being of others.

A savior complex can be subtle, and the person who has such a self-image can be unaware of it, simply because the behaviors can appear to have good motives and can be beneficial to others. Suffice it to say, we need to do what we are asked to do by others, and we need to *not* do what they don't want us to do. We need to grant others freedom to make their own choices and to live their own lives. I, as a healing presence, walk with others in their pain and in their joy. I don't take on their suffering in a futile effort to make them feel better. It doesn't work.

Empathy provides energy to others because it makes them aware that we understand their suffering and don't judge, condemn, or try to fix their problems. Sympathy, by contrast, takes on the feelings and pain of others in an effort to identify with their plight. (*Sympathy* here is used in its current cultural context. Linguistically, sympathy can connote compassion, but it generally means non-compassion in today's world.)

A person who is a healing presence to another person provides empathy in abundance without accepting or expressing sympathy. Sympathy for another person simply magnifies the problem. Sympathy is codependence and pride in disguise. If someone else is feeling depressed, it doesn't do him or her any good if I become sympathetic and take on the depressed feelings. Other people need hope and strength, not another depressed person to pull them deeper into darkness.

Active Listening to Enrich Others

"LISTENING IS LOVE DELIVERED." This statement is axiomatic in family life and when visiting a patient in the hospital. Perhaps it is even more so during serious discussions about becoming a healing presence for others.

I converted to Orthodoxy thirty-three years ago, and I owe my very life and such sanity as I have to the Church. I firmly believe that the Orthodox Church has "the fullness of the truth," and we need to do all we can to cherish what we have been given.

During my work on many committees and commissions in the Orthodox Church, active listening has been part of, and sometimes absent from, the deliberations. As a member of the now extinct SCOBA Committee on Social and Moral Issues for many years, I had the enriching experience of working with members of other jurisdictions who actually listened to each other. Yes, the meetings were sometimes long and tense. Yes, I learned an immense amount about all the social and moral issues of the day. Some of my most prized convictions were

challenged, and changed, by the interactions and honest dialogue. I am forever grateful for the experience of working with
other Orthodox Christians who had the love and the sanity to
listen to each other and speak from their heart.

This has not been the norm in some of my other committee and one-on-one exchanges about serious church matters.
Sometimes I have felt that the other person had an opinion and
was merely tolerating my ideas until he or she could present the
other side. And I have no doubt that I have not always been a
paragon of active listening. Lord, have mercy. We all have much
to learn.

Becoming a healing presence requires attentiveness to the
needs of others, especially those who live and work closely
with us.

The Orthodox Church Today

WE NEED TO FACE SQUARELY the facts of the Orthodox
Church today. We are steadily being challenged by new moral
standards in contemporary culture. Words like *marriage* and
adult have new connotations. Virtually all the established main-
line churches are experiencing the same issues, but that is of
little comfort. The question is, "Where do we go from here?"
Two things are certain. First, we can no longer do "business as
usual." Second, we need to work together. There is no other way.

I am convinced that if we learn from each other how and when to actively listen, we can move Christ's Church in an evangelical direction. If we listen to Christ speaking to us through each other, Christ in us can empower us to do His work better.

Active Listening Defined

WHAT IS ACTIVE LISTENING? Active listening is being attentive to the basic meaning and the feelings in a statement made by another. Active listening absorbs the meanings and feelings behind the other's words *and* demonstrates, to the satisfaction of the other, that we actually heard what was said. Our response is usually a short declarative sentence.

Active listening is not judgmental or critical or patronizing or advice-giving. Active listening does not try to fix problems. It is simply being fully present to the other as the other speaks *and* showing the other person that we heard what was said.

An Orthodox man told me he was having a particularly difficult week. He said a friend asked him how he was doing, and he replied, "My life is like a roller coaster." To his surprise, his friend gave a little sermonette about life. Looking for some strength and hope, he told another friend the same thing: "My life is like a roller coaster." Again he was met with a stone wall of glib words. Active listening as love delivered can be in short supply sometimes, even within Orthodoxy.

And active listening, at its best, doesn't ask many questions. Some questions for clarification are okay, but questions can be a way of controlling the conversation and the other person. When I ask a question, I put the other person in the position of having to either answer or ignore my question. If we aren't careful, questions easily slip into interrogation. Adolescents often hate questions precisely because they sniff out the power differential between the questioner and the person being questioned. But, again, a few questions are acceptable during active listening.

In *The Brothers Karamazov*, Father Zossima provides a deep insight for us:

> *"At some ideas you stand perplexed, especially at the sight of men's sins, asking yourself whether to combat it by force or by humble love. Always decide, 'I will combat it by humble love.' If you make up your mind about that, once and for all, you may be able to conquer the whole world. Loving humility is an awesome force, the strongest of all, and there is nothing like it."*

When my daughter was a teenager, we had the same scene at the dinner table for many evenings. I was preoccupied with making the family meal a "quality time" experience. I would ask my wife how her day was, and we would engage in banter and conversation. I then asked Timothy, the younger child, about his day, and he became lively as he described it. Then I asked my teen, Beth, what she did that day. She replied crisply, "Work and play." But I didn't get it. I didn't get the message that she didn't like being questioned.

Finally, when I asked what she did one day, she said, "W and P." She was no longer willing to give me even the full words—just the initials. Well, I learned my lesson. Beth could be very disclosing and talkative about her life when she wanted to be. I call her my champagne bubble. However, when pinned with a direct question when she didn't feel like answering, she would eloquently clam up.

Active listening to another when the other wants to be heard is an act of love. Direct questions can sometimes be invasive, particularly with adolescents.

> *Active listening to another when the other wants to be heard is an act of love.*

And, of course, we need to express our opinion honestly and candidly. But we can only do this constructively—that is, be listened to—if we have earned our way into the conversation by listening first. That's often the rub. Many of us simply don't want to, or can't, listen first. That can sink our relational Titanic.

Jury Duty

I HAD A SURPRISING EXPERIENCE of active listening when I was on jury duty. After days of honest and contentious debate we, the jury, came to an impasse. We began saying the same things, only louder. People got up and walked around the small jury room, exasperated.

Then I suggested we try an exercise. I asked that we indicate who thought the defendant was guilty and who thought she was innocent. The group was split, six to three. Then I asked the group who thought the defendant was guilty to gather in a corner, take an hour, and make a case that she was innocent. Then I asked those who thought she was innocent to gather in the other corner and make a case that she was guilty. I said the purpose wasn't to convince the other group, but simply to demonstrate that we were listening to each other and understood the opposing opinion. A spokesperson from each group would make a report after an hour.

The jury broke into two groups and, after an hour, reconvened. Fascinatingly, some votes changed, including my own. More importantly, the atmosphere in the room changed dramatically as soon as we began the exercise. The mood in the room, which had been tense and adversarial, became light and jovial. One person called out, "You think you have a difficult job. We are making your case for you." Everyone laughed. In the end, we came to a consensus with grateful unanimity. The old-timers on the jury said they had never experienced such a dramatic turnaround and such a satisfying ending.

The point is, when we begin to fully listen we begin to be open to new spaces in our hearts for others to influence us and for us to influence others. As Stephen Covey said, "Seek first to understand, then to be understood."[34] That *sequence* needs to be our common marching order as we move forward, in the Spirit, to work in Christ's vineyard.

We listen before we speak. We seek to discern the uniqueness of the other person's meaning before we comment.

---

34 Stephen R. Covey, *The 7 Habits of Highly Effective People* (New York: Simon & Schuster, 1989), p. 235.

CHAPTER 6

Surrender

WE BEGIN BY TURNING TO CHRIST, who said, "Love one another as I have loved you." The huge challenge rests in the word *as*. We do that by encountering others and giving them Christ's strength and hope. It is both fascinating and humbling to know that He wants to allow His fire of healing to flow through us to others.

Surrender as Victory

WE ALLOW HIS FIRE TO FLOW through us to others by surrendering our ego and accepting His fire in us. Surrender is not defeat. On the contrary, surrender is victory in and through Christ.

Surrender is not flat or dull or capitulating. It can be filled with music, wonder, awe. Surrender is a receptive engagement with the present moment, much like a bride awaiting her bridegroom. Christ is our Bridegroom. In Orthodoxy we sing and hear the music of surrender: "Behold the Bridegroom cometh" begins Lent, a time of preparation and surrender by fasting so that we can become lean and receptive.

We surrender our desires so that we unite to each other at a deeper level. I recall overhearing my married daughter, Beth, say to her husband, "I don't care where we go on vacation as long as I am with you." She surrendered her preference for a vacation for the opportunity to unite to her husband in love. So, too, with our relationship with Christ. We might say to the Lord, "I don't care where I go today as long as I am with You."

That's what it's all about. It's about us becoming musical, becoming music, becoming a new creation.

> *We surrender our ego to heal others.*

The way to have more to give others is to have less of ourselves, our expectations, plans, and agendas. We surrender our ego to heal others. This is a variant of John the Forerunner's words, "He must increase and I must decrease." My neighbor—friend or stranger—must increase in my mind; then I automatically think less of myself. I choose to fill my mind with more than my own predilections, desires, and wants.

This is called surrender of the self. Surrender is not passive but active. Surrender is opening my hands and heart to be filled by God.

Clearly, this understanding of surrender is countercultural.

Generally, the culture defines surrender in terms of a loser and a winner. However, according to the Christian understanding of surrender, when I surrender my ego, I win and the other person wins. Surrender is a win-win situation.

We don't control our interactions with other humans. God does. St. Barsanuphius said, "Do not forget that without God there is no healing for anyone."[35] There is *no* healing. None. None without God. Although this may seem to be common sense, St. Barsanuphius's words are profound.

I am reminded of the evangelical teenager who met her ex-pastor at the shopping mall. The pastor said, "Diane, I haven't seen you in church for a while. Is anything going on?"

Diane responded, "I am not going back to any church ever again. You pastors all say the same thing."

The rather baffled pastor said, "Diane, in the last four years you have been in three different churches. How can we pastors all be saying the same thing?"

"It all comes down to this, however you say it: A. God is good. B. I am bad. C. Try harder. It doesn't work, and I am outta there."

Diane is absolutely right. That pastor's approach is the opposite of authentic Christianity. Diane

> *We try harder to not try harder.*

---

35 Jean-Claude Larche, *Theology of Illness* (Crestwood, NY: SVS Press, 2002), p. 117.

has the pulse of the Truth. Authentic Christianity, and therefore authentic helping and healing, is the opposite. We try
harder to *not* try harder. We try to learn to let go and let God
do for us what we can't do for ourselves. That's the heart of the
matter. It's not as if I did something stupendous; I helped and
healed somebody. So?

We Westerners, especially in the United States, have an
ingrained propensity to measure our lives by our achieve-
ments. We do some good and expect some reward. We fail
at a project and expect a punishment. We think we earn our
"grace," so to speak. We feel we have somehow behaved in a
way that pleases God and therefore we "stand in good stead."
We performed well and will receive a pat on the head, a special
favor with God, and eventually, after a lifetime of Christian
living, we "get" heaven.

But this performance mentality obstructs the possibility of
being poor, needy, and loved simply because we are God's children. Grace is a free gift, not something we earn or deserve. Yes,
we must do our part, but our part is to
accept the gift and to say, like the Theotokos, "Be it done to me according to
Thy Word."

> For the
> Christian,
> a self-made
> man is an
> oxymoron.

A statue called *Self-Made Man* by
Bobbie Carlyle eloquently portrays our
plight. It renders a man in an upright
block of stone. The bottom half of the

block is untouched, a pillar of solid rock. The upper half of the statue represents a muscular and fierce man bending over the stone with a chisel and mallet in his hand. He is chiseling the bottom half of his body from the uncut stone. He is diligently working to free himself from his prison of rock and become "himself." He is carving his character, carving his future. The man is freeing his stone leg from the block of stone. For the Christian, a self-made man is an oxymoron.

The *Self-Made Man* stands forever "making himself." In one sense, the statue vividly depicts the truth that we must work hard at our entire life, especially our spiritual life: we must work hard at being still and at constantly being aware of the presence of Christ. Spirituality is about seeing and, above all else, about a relationship with Christ. But the self-made person is eternally stuck in the plight of doomed self-creation.[36]

God makes us. We don't make ourselves. The genius of the portrayal is its depiction of the futility of the self-made man's effort. He is his own artist, his own sculptor, his own creator. The man expends utmost effort trying to finish "his work," making himself in his own image and likeness, yet never becoming his own god.

---

36   The statue can be viewed at http://www.bobbiecarlylesculpture. com.

Unexpected Moments

A FEW YEARS AGO I had an interesting experience at a St. Vladimir's Seminary Institute. I was scheduled to give a morning talk. After Matins I tried to catch Father Tom Hopko; he is my spiritual father, and I wanted his blessing to hand out a quote from St. Theophan, already printed out on handouts. When I approached him, he was speaking with a woman, so I waited. When he finished, I said, "Father Tom, I have a quote I would like to share with you."

He said, "No, Al, I have a quote I want to share with you."

"No, I have to give a talk in ten minutes downstairs."

"Well, Al, then just listen to the quote I want to give you now."

Of course, I said okay. He opened the book he was holding, *The Art of Prayer*, and read the exact quote I was holding in my hand. Chills went up my spine. Of all the books Father Tom has in his library and of all the quotes in *The Art of Prayer*, he read me the quote that I then handed him. I don't want to make more of this than it is. It is what it is. But the coincidence for me was mind-blowing. And, of course, we Orthodox don't believe in coincidences.

Here is the quote from St. Theophan, which is powerful to me to this day:

> *Seek God, such is the unalterable rule of all spiritual advancement. Nothing comes without effort. The help of God is always*

ready and always near, but it is only given to those who seek and work, and only to those who put their own powers to the test, then cry out with all their heart: Lord, help us. So long as you hold on to even a little hope of achieving something by your own powers, the Lord does not interfere. It is as though He says, "You hope to succeed by yourself—very well, go on trying. But, however long you try, you will achieve nothing." May the Lord give you a contrite spirit, a humble and contrite heart.[37]

That's the point. We can achieve nothing—and certainly will not help another at all—by ourselves. In fact, when we try to help by ourselves, we often end up doing more harm than good. But when we surrender to Christ, all things are possible with Him.

This distinction is subtle but vital. It is the difference between doing something on my own steam and following the lead of the Lord and doing His desire.

My daughter, Beth, who is now married and has three children, spent a semester during college in Siena, Italy, doing research. She stayed with a family and became like a daughter to them. As her term-paper project, she did a study of the baptistery in the Siena Cathedral. The cathedrals in Siena and Florence, about fifty miles apart, were both begun in the thirteenth century and took centuries to complete. They were built competitively: When one of the cathedrals occupied more ground, the other expanded its nave. When one raised its roof, the other built a tower. Over the decades, the competition deteriorated

---

37 Chariton of Valamo, comp., *The Art of Prayer* (London: Faber & Faber, 1977), p. 133.

into darkness. Ugly tales are still told about the building of the two neighboring cathedrals. Both cathedrals are ravishingly beautiful and majestic. Gorgeous to the eye. Magnificent structures.

Beth finished studying the baptistery in the Siena Cathedral to her satisfaction. She then decided to take a bus on a Sunday afternoon and visit the Florence Cathedral to see what it was like. Beth told the woman she was staying with about her plan, and the woman said flatly, "If you go to Florence to see their cathedral, don't ever come back to this house again." She was dead serious.

The hatred from centuries ago lives on to this day in some who live in Siena and perhaps in Florence as well. Both cathedrals are radiant, but we might ponder whether they give God all the glory they could. The point is clear. If we build or do anything from our own motives, we are probably building or doing something counterproductive, and probably in vain.

Ask to Receive

IF WE TRY TO LEARN to surrender but seem baffled by the entire approach, where do we start? We start where the Lord told us to start. He said, "Ask, and it will be given to you; seek, and you will find; knock, and it will be opened to you" (Matt. 7:7). Jesus is not stingy with light or strength, especially if we ask how to become a healing presence for others. But our little part is to ask and ask and ask. That is, we try to live in His presence and take our cues from Him. We say, "May Your desires be done through me. Not my desires but Yours be done."

In the quote Fr. Hopko read to me, the person in the quote was hoping to achieve something by his own powers. It simply doesn't work. We can learn to try to not try so hard. As St. Irenaeus said, "We relax in God's hands."

> *St. Irenaeus said, "We relax in God's hands."*

Or, as St. Gregory the Theologian said, "It is necessary to be at ease to know God."

How often should we ask? Once I was at an Al-Anon meeting, and a woman simply said, "I ask God for directions about a hundred times a day." I must admit that, at that moment, I was extremely judgmental of her. I didn't say anything out loud, but I thought, *What a compulsive nut.* That was fifteen years ago. Today I ask God for directions many times, perhaps a hundred times a day. So, by God's grace and the influence of many people, I have become the compulsive nut I mentally accused the woman of being. And, of course, asking God a hundred times a day is not compulsive but rather is a lovely relationship of creature to Creator.

As Metropolitan Kallistos Ware reminds us, we need to understand that "gradualness is necessary—an orderly ascent from exterior to interior deeds."[38] We have to work and strive. We have to do our part. But our efforts need to be fueled and directed by hearing God's voice, following His beckoning through our heart, striving to surrender to Him in ourselves and in others. We need to give time, time.

All this has to do with whether we are effective mutual healers in our lives *together*. Many of us have trouble with this. Researchers did an interesting study of missionaries of all denominations who returned prematurely—that is, before their expected date of return. The researchers gave the missionaries a list of ten possible reasons for returning and asked the missionaries to rank them from one to ten. The list included such items as "couldn't learn the language" and "found the living conditions to be unsatisfactory." The number-one reason given, by far, was "the presence of other Christian missionaries." We understand what is being said in that research. The missionaries came back because they couldn't live in a foreign country with other Christian missionaries.

That is an astounding finding. The returning missionaries said, in effect, that the greatest barrier to spreading Christ's Word was the presence of their fellow Christian missionaries. We have much to learn from that study, because the conclusions have a generalized application. Perhaps one of the great hindrances to the spread of Orthodoxy today is our own impact on our fellow Orthodox believers, and then on others who see

---

38 Chariton, *The Art of Prayer*, p. 17.

this. And then the effect cascades onto others who see it all. That thought can give us pause.

We can better learn to become a healing presence as we learn to open ourselves more to the music of the Bridegroom and to ask for more grace. "Lord, I surrender myself to You to do with me as You will. Grant that I may become a healing presence to others."

CHAPTER 7

The Sacrament of the Present Moment

The Present Moment Is Explosive

METROPOLITAN KALLISTOS WARE talks about the sacrament of the present moment. He explains that the present moment is the point at which time touches eternity.

It is fascinating that a number of Orthodox theologians choose the word *sacrament* when writing about the present moment. The Orthodox understanding of *sacrament* is a mystery, which is more than a sign but rather "something becoming what it is," "a dynamic synthesis of symbol and fulfillment."[39]

A metaphor for mystery might be incense. Incense is beautiful, fragrant, rises to high heaven, and is known sensually, yet is beyond our grasp. We can't grasp incense or incense smoke,

---

39 Alexander Schmemann, *For the Life of the World* (Crestwood, NY: St. Vladimir's Seminary Press, 1973), pp. 26, 151.

> *Our task is to be faithful to the present moment.*

yet incense takes us to a deeper experience of what is real, what is really going on. Mystery.

In a sense, speaking about the present moment can be ho-hum because we know that we ought to live in the present moment but aren't very good at it. Talking about the present moment can be like "do good and avoid evil." Self-evident. Yet the more we open our minds to new levels of the importance of the present moment, the more chance we have of "getting there." We only "get there," or better said, "get here," by settling down and becoming centered. The present moment is quietly explosive, combustible with the very presence of God. Our task is to be faithful to the present moment—that is, to have an unconditional interest in it.

Interestingly, we can be a healing presence only in the present moment. There is no other place to go. This requires focused attentiveness to the present moment and the person in front of us. As St. Simeon the New Theologian said, "Do not worry about what will come next; you will discover it when it comes."

At the beginning of our marriage I recall my wife saying to me, "Al, I would like to spend one day inside your head." Somehow she thought that I had an interesting adventure going on in my cranium. Wrong. I told her I wouldn't wish that on her in a million years. Inside my head, as is the case with all sinful humans I know, an intense spiritual warfare is continually going on. The temptations are sometimes vile and corrupt, to be fought and conquered. I would not have wanted my wife to be privy to my private battles. I loved her too much. In the present moment we can gain victory over the spiritual warfare and try to be a calming presence, despite the inner turmoil.

Archimandrite Meletios Webber speaks eloquently of the mystery of the present moment:

> *We can only meet God in the present moment. This is an area where God chooses to put limits on His own power. We choose whether or not to live in the present moment. . . . We can only make decisions in the present moment. We can only enjoy sights and sounds in the present moment. We can only love or hate, sing or cry, in the present moment. Of all the possible points in time, only the present moment is available for repentance.*
>
> *The present moment may appear to be tiny in duration—so much so that the human mind thinks it hardly exists at all—but in depth it is beyond infinite. Actually, it has no shape or form. That's one of the problems. There is nothing to measure here, and that really infuriates the mind since measurement is what the mind is good at. The present moment is formless and may be experienced as large or small. If we are sitting in the dentist's chair and the dentist hits a nerve, then time seems large. If, however, we are having a very enjoyable gourmet meal, then time may seem to pass like a blink. . . . In some senses the present moment is of almost no duration. None at all. In other ways, it is eternal life. Whichever we choose, it is nevertheless the only space within which we can operate. It's odd that we don't spend more time in the present moment than we do. Unfortunately, the*

mind blocks the availability of the present moment whenever it has a chance to do so.

The mind, the rational mind, cannot trust the present moment since it cannot control it. Of course, we are rational beings and we need our rational mind, the forehead, the cerebral cortex. But, regarding the present moment, the mind is almost always at enmity with it. The mind cannot control the present moment, the time during which things can arise, so the mind pretends that it does not exist. This causes a person to behave in a completely unconscious way, way down, rather like an octopus flailing about in many directions. This forces the person to wait for the mind to absorb an event, which by then has become an event in the past, before she or he is allowed to experience it. One of the important functions of prayer is to bring us into, and to assist us to remain in, the present moment.[40]

The present moment is an opportunity or a burden. We are free to choose our attitude about the present moment, making the moment a joy or a hindrance.

Ways into the Present Moment

WHAT CAN WE FIND to assist us in our quest to enter the present moment more fully? Prayer is the perfect way. Beyond prayer, there are at least three basic ways, all of which have to do with altering our awareness. First, we can be attentive to our breath and our heartbeat. When I am aware of my breathing,

---

40 Meletios Webber, *Bread & Water, Wine & Oil* (Ben Lomond, CA: Conciliar Press, 2007), p. 80.

I can't be aware of my past or my future. I am simply aware of my breathing. Of course, this harkens to previous chapters and the profound words of the desert fathers. When we focus on our breath and heartbeat, we focus on our inner body, our inner universe, where Christ resides.

Second, we can choose to be more aware of the specifics of our current environment. We can notice if the room is warm or chilly. Does the time seem to be moving slowly or quickly? Are there any distant sounds, such as those of birds?

Third, we can become more aware of our bodily sensations, the distinctiveness of this moment's "data" as awareness of our bodies. For example, is the pen I'm holding thin or thick? Can I feel my toes move in my shoes? Do my facial muscles feel relaxed or taut? One practical thing to do is be more aware of one's fingertips. I can run my fingertips across the cloth in front of me, being aware of its texture.

One implication of these insights is what is called in the secular culture "living in the power of the now." We can begin with each new and fresh breath. Each breath has been preplanned by God to be part of the larger mosaic of our life. No breath is wasted or negligible. We treasure each new breath until our last. We treasure each breath with the awareness that our breath—

> *We can begin with each new and fresh breath.*

that is, life—is given to us to become a healing presence for others and ourselves.

When I go to international conventions, I often hear about the importance of each breath. If I go into secular bookstores, I find these insights in bestselling books. The present breath is the portal to the present moment, the power of the now. And that is the only place where God is. That can be a conversation stopper or starter, even in non-Christian circles. But the secular culture does not have a monopoly on insights into the value of the present moment. The Church Fathers and the wise theologians explain the present moment eloquently.

When we are in the present moment, even for a short time, we can simultaneously experience time as standing still and as a rhythmic flow. Time is standing still, but it is not a photograph, not a static, dead thing. Rather, it is the living paradox of two realities concurrently. For example, I used to downhill ski all day and would end up feeling half-frozen. When I got in the car and turned the heater to high, I experienced being cold and warm at the same time. The inside of my body was still cold, but the outside had become warm. Living with paradox, especially a physical paradox, can be jarring and freeing, a paradox in itself.

> *When we are faithful to the present moment, we can feel rooted.*

When we are faithful to the present moment, we can

feel rooted, as if our feet are growing roots into the ground. We feel stabilized.

Living in the Now

A RUSSIAN JOKE helps us keep our perspective: "The future is ensured. It's just the past that keeps changing."

Fr. Alexander Schmemann spoke glowingly of drinking orange juice as a human act that paralleled the Eucharist. He spoke about savoring the orange juice, making the ordinary act into a sacred act. Savoring and cherishing are part of taking delight in the present moment.

A colleague made a memorable statement as we walked across campus to our respective offices one day: "All I have to do is walk from here to my office and *not* do the 102 projects awaiting me on my desktop." I don't have to do *now* the many projects awaiting my attention. We don't have to carry all those projects now. My tendency, and perhaps yours, is to want to hold all my projects in my head now and work on all of them at the same time as I am walking across campus, or anywhere else.

We looked at three ways to increase our power of living in the moment. The primary way to center ourselves is prayer. Prayer can be a fine entrée into the present moment. When we are in prayer, we are not into our floating stream of consciousness. Within the prayer comes the power of Christ, a power that softens our heart and brings serenity, at least for a short while and perhaps longer. Am I writing with attention and breathing with serenity? Am I typing at the computer with calm, or am I hurrying and making many mistakes?

An Orthodox bishop recommended to me a book about contemplation: *A Sunlit Absence* by Martin Laird. I certainly would recommend the book to anyone interested in contemplation. Laird says, "The present moment has an utterly reliable way of being exactly the way it is at any given moment. . . . The present moment reveals the 'sunlit absence,' life as firm and unshakable as it is an ungraspable flow; unshakable because it is our foundation; ungraspable, because it is constantly being poured out as a pure gift."[41]

> *The present is the*
> *point at which*
> *time touches*
> *eternity.*

God wants men to attend chiefly to two things: to eternity itself, and to that point in time where we contact eternity.

The present is the point at which time touches eternity. Of the present moment, and of it only, humans have the experience God has of reality as a whole; in it alone freedom and actuality are offered to them. When we are alive in the current moment, we are a walking Christmas Day, a continual rebirth-

---

41 Martin Laird, *A Sunlit Absence* (New York: Oxford University Press, 2011), p. 76.

ing of the Lord into the universe. In the person who dwells in a present *now*, God begets His Son without ceasing.

Paul Evdokimov, said, "The hour through which you are at present passing, the man whom you meet here and now, the task on which you are engaged at this very moment—these are always the most important in your whole life." Is that really true? Is it true that what I am doing right now, menial as it may seem, is the most important moment of my life? Yes.

Hence, God has you and me right where He wants you and me. This is hugely liberating. We don't have to analyze, squint and squirm, or figure everything out. Nope. Quite the opposite. Ruskin's coat of arms says it all: "Today, today, today."[42]

Our choice is not a once-for-all declaration, "I'm going to live in the present moment." Rather, our choice is a provisional affirmation that will be strengthened and altered by the next set of circumstances God sends when we may suddenly get a little headache or a weird memory. Then we make a new decision, experience a new softening, and become a new person or a "new creation" (2 Cor. 5:17).

The Greek philosophers were fond of saying that we never step into the same stream twice. We put our foot into the stream and take it out. We put the foot back into the stream, but during the interval, our foot has changed, the stream has changed, and so has the flow of the present moment.

---

42   Kallistos Ware, *The Orthodox Way* (Crestwood, NY: St. Vladimir's Seminary Press, 2002), p. 153.

St. Hesychios said, "The continuity of attention [i.e. the present moment] produces inner stability; inner stability produces . . . watchfulness and in due measure gives contemplative insight into spiritual warfare."

Redeeming Time

WE ALWAYS, ALWAYS begin with Christ and His Word. We find in Ephesians, "See that you walk circumspectly . . . redeeming the time" (Eph. 5:15–16). That's our job, to redeem the time. Christ is our Way and Truth and Life, and in that sense, our Time. He redeems time through us.

The Orthodox meaning of time gives us the freedom to love, to take the risk to love. Time and eternity are different; they are not mutually exclusive but complementary. We are not to become timeless but to transfigure time. Some of our common expressions give us a view into how we can misuse time, such as "killing time" or "wasting time" or even "saving time."

Time isn't ours to fritter away or to save. Time is ours to transform and transfigure. So the meaning of time is found in the risk of love, in relationships, in response and openness to the other. Of course, our basic relationship is with Jesus Christ. We try to use our God-given time to be as aware and

> *Time is ours to transform and transfigure.*

connected with Him as we can and then to do what He has put us on the planet to do. Time is a gift to become more of a healing presence.

For my birthday, my children bought me a wall clock, especially "for Dad," their rather compulsive father. The clock, a beautiful thing, is about eight inches by eight inches. It is white ceramic with a black wooden frame and black moving hands. In the bottom left corner of the clock are the black numbers, all mumbo jumbo, with the eight on top of the two and the five. There are no numbers making a circle around the hands to indicate the time. On the top of the clock, where the number 12 is usually placed, is the word *Whatever*.

It's the main clock in my little apartment. And it's the clock I tell time by. When I look up at it, I see the *Whatever* as I try to discover the time of day. That's my children's way of saying, "Relax, Dad. Let go and let God."

We Orthodox use two Greek words to describe time: *chronos* and *kairos*. Chronos refers to measured time: Tuesday follows Monday, July precedes August. We need measured time to be able to think, communicate, and live rationally. Kairos is God's time, God's eternal moment in the chronos. We try, as much as we can, to keep those two aspects of time in mind.

An Orthodox philosophy of time differs from secular philosophies. For example, Plato presented an idea of time that is circular. Time revolves on itself. What happens has a beginning and ending, all moving in a circular way. The secular world, by contrast, explains time exclusively in terms of chronos, linear, 24/7 and 365. That's time, tick, tick, tick. It simply goes along, inexorably, in a straight line.

An Orthodox view of time is cruciform. All events that happened before the Cross, for the Christian, led up to the Cross. All. Subsequently, all events after the Cross are defined by the Cross and look back to the Cross for meaning. So the Cross is the center of time; it magnifies and gives perspective to time.

Time as cruciform is a valid model for history, the larger picture, and is also valid for our personal lives, the smaller picture. In my life, all that has preceded this moment has led up to the Cross as my salvation at this moment. All the time I have left on this planet goes back to the Cross. The Cross organizes my time, giving meaning to my personal time.

Time has a depth and profundity for Christians that the philosophers and the secularists can't grasp, because it is all based in Christ and His saving action for us on the Cross.

For Orthodox Christians, time—for example, 2:30 in the afternoon on a Tuesday—is basically a spiritual issue. It's not about the control of our time but the surrender of it. We begin by saying that time is a gift from God that we are called to accept and use properly. Like all other gifts of health, friendship, and breath, we cherish time as a great gift bestowed on us by a loving God.

We rejoice in time. We splash in time. We are grateful for the time we have, no more and no less. A friend told me recently,

"Time is our friend." It occurred to me that time can be our friend or our enemy, depending on our perspective. Time is either for us or against us. For some of us, at some points in our day, particularly in the late afternoon when our blood sugar is low, it can be difficult to perceive time as a friend.

We use time prudently when we go inward to be aware of the presence of Christ and then go outward to be a healing presence to others. In the time we have remaining on the earth, we share our time and ourselves to give others strength and hope.

Time Management

THE FIRST THING TO SAY about time management is that there is no such thing. We don't "manage" time. Time manages us if we allow the Lord to have a place in our schedule.

Christ is everything, including the Lord and owner of our time. He is the Way, the how, the format, the prioritizing of our schedule.

C. S. Lewis said we usually regard time as our own. We start our day with the curious assumption that we are the lawful possessors of an upcoming twenty-four hours. With that hazardous assumption, we fill the matrix of our day with slots of tasks or restful moments. We might hope that we are somehow planning our time in a way that pleases God. But, when we begin with the assumption that time is ours, then inconveniences, particularly people who appear before us wanting strength and hope, can become intrusions into our afternoon.[43]

The assumption is probably in large part unconscious. I might get up, pray, have a cup of coffee, and look down the highway at what this day looks like to me—what *my* day looks like to me.

By contrast, we can begin with the assertion that our time is not our own but the Lord's. We adjust our expectations. We ask, "Lord, what do You want me to do now?" Better said, "Lord, what do You want to do through me now? What kind of fire do you want to bring through my behaviors that will eventually make me more of a healing presence for others?" This removes the emphasis on the ego and places it on the Lord, thus making us free and peaceful. If interruptions come, and they will, they can be perceived as coming directly from the hand of God. If we are sensitive to each moment as God's moment, we can be grateful for interruptions, because God often moves in unexpected ways.

Our freedom consists in embracing all that happens to us, negative and positive, pain and pleasure, disappointment and joy, as a blessing in divine disguise. Metropolitan Philaret's prayer has been quoted often: "In unforeseen events let us not forget that all are sent by You."

We need to push "pause" often and avoid reacting to the

---

43   C. S. Lewis, *The Screwtape Letters* (New York: Harper One, 1996), p. 21.

latest and loudest. Rather, we need to remember Jesus and then gain some perspective on what He wants us to do next. The Lord expects us to live a life of love for Him and for others.

> *We don't live life. Life lives us.*

We have all the time we need to do all the things God has us here to do, in a peaceful way. God is not stingy with time. We revere time as a way to remain peaceful, no matter what, to please God who gave us time. We have time to become more of a healing presence during our remaining time on earth.

We don't live life. Life lives us.

CHAPTER 8

Suffering and Death

Becoming a healing presence implies healing from something—healing from suffering.

Why do children suffer from leukemia? Why did my wife suffer as she did with metastasized bone cancer, with pain that morphine couldn't touch? Why do people suffer? It's a profound question, the answer to which we just don't know. We will never adequately comprehend or teach the meaning of suffering.

We look to the Bible. As it says in Isaiah 55:8–9,

> *"For My thoughts are not your thoughts,*
> *Nor are your ways My ways," says the* Lord.
> *"For as the heavens are higher than the earth,*
> *So are My ways higher than your ways,*
> *And My thoughts than your thoughts."*

We begin with the clear awareness that we don't have easy, cheap words to give to others about suffering, particularly pertaining to the future. We certainly don't say things are going to get better. We have no idea what the future holds. How can we say that the future will be better? On a human level, things might get much worse. So we don't pretend to have answers for others about suffering.

Suffering is universal. However, Christian believers do have a unique perspective on the meaning of suffering. We begin with the claim that for the believer, suffering has meaning. It depends on how we perceive the suffering. How we deal with suffering makes all the difference. The Lord said that the Father makes His sun rise on the evil and on the good, and He sends rain on the just and on the unjust (Matt. 5:45).

> *For the believer, suffering has meaning.*

There are two kinds of suffering: meaningful or meaningless. Suffering that is meaningful for the Christian believer is redemptive. Christ suffered for us to save us, to help us, to heal us. He allows His followers to suffer to participate in His Way, in the healing of those around them. Christ said the disciple is not above the Master. So, for the believer, suffering has a redemptive aspect—that is, my suffering can and does do good for others; it helps and heals. That is a mystery, and it's an astounding Christian claim. Astounding and valid.

This truth can be useful to those who are suffering horribly, especially people in nursing homes who are lonely and wonder why God doesn't just take them to heaven. They might ask, "Why am I sitting here with rheumatoid arthritis? Why doesn't

God just take me?" The answer is that God is God. His ways are not our ways. Those in nursing homes or afflicted seriously in any way might be helped if they can understand that their suffering has meaning. A believer's suffering can help her children and grandchildren as well as those who live in the same nursing home.

No doubt, any form of suffering poses difficulty. Solzhenitsyn said we have three choices: We can give up. We can give in. We can go on. The Christian chooses to go on in the light of faith that there is more to suffering than suffering itself.

> *We can give up. We can give in. We can go on.*

Suffering can be meaningless, or worse, if we choose not to see God's hand present with us. Suffering can become an interior cancer, eating us alive as it metastasizes on its own darkness.

It is well known in social agencies that "hurt people hurt people"—that is, people who have been hurt, particularly those who were abused during childhood, tend to hurt others when they become adults. We might like to think the opposite. We might like to think that people who were abused in childhood know the pain and suffering of the abuse, so they would not want to hurt others because they know from experience the ravages of the hurt. Alas, statistically, such is not the case. There are exceptions, but exceptions they are.

We live in a sinful, fallen world that is messy and filled with horrors of various kinds. And, yes, our world is beautiful and filled with people of courage and compassion as well. There are many people who choose to become healing presences for others.

My wife suffered from bone cancer. She agonized for a very long time. Why? I don't pretend to know. What I do know is that her suffering did benefit me and our children and grandchildren greatly. My daughter, particularly, says that all the good in her life now, decades after her mother died, has come through her mother.

Understanding suffering is a very important part of our understanding of becoming a healing presence. We may not be able to alleviate suffering, but we can try to provide a loving presence to others in their suffering. We can try to walk with people in their suffering.

My wife would greet me at the door at the end of my day's work with the words, "Al, I'm glad you weren't hit by a truck." So her definition of a good day for me meant that I didn't get hit by a truck. She knew me well. The only reason a truck didn't hit me was because my guardian angel diverted the trucks from my path. But, tragically, some wives do have husbands who are hit by a truck, leaving them with small children to raise and no insurance. How do we account for such inequities? We don't. We simply try to be humble enough to know that there are some—no, many—questions we can't answer.

But we do know that we have a choice. We can either become

angry, bitter, and self-pitying or we can work through the suffering by expressing some sort of faith.

The healing power of our suffering comes through our poverty. There are many losses, such as the loss of memory or loss of a child, that cannot be overcome or understood.

Suffering can be a form of prayer. Sometimes all we can do is nod in God's direction, wordless and emotionless. Even such a nod toward God is a call to Him, a prayer.

We can ask the question, "Why do bad things happen to good people?" A better question might be, "Why don't more bad things happen to good people?" The question has to do with expectations.

And the disciple is not above the Master. Jesus' disciples were maltreated, and bad things did happen to them shortly after Jesus' death and through the centuries.

God did not create suffering, evil, or death. To questions like, "Did God send the planes into the World Trade Center in New York City?" the clear answer is, "No, humans flew the planes into the World Trade Center."

All of us suffer. Our sufferings are not unknown to Christ and can be of great benefit to others and ourselves. We can become a healing presence simply by being alive, believing as best we can, and offering our sufferings to Christ.

We are especially loved by the Lord when we are poor and suffering. That's why He came. He breathes, speaks, and provides a message to others through us. That's the way the Lord works. He chooses the poor and the suffering to do His bidding, His healing on this earth.

Death

If we are going to be a healing presence to others and ourselves, we need to be clear about our attitude toward the ultimate reality—namely, death.

> *A perfect sense of death is free from fear.*

"The fathers assert that perfect love is sinless, and it seems to me that a perfect sense of death is free from fear."[44] Well, that attitude is a goal many of us, myself included, have not reached. But at least we Orthodox have a guideline.

Every death and every grieving about death involves a loss of some sort. Death is synonymous with separation.

Our brain consists of a hundred billion cells, give or take a couple of billion. Ten thousand of those cells die every day. We aren't conscious of the process of losing brain cells. One day blurs into the next as life goes on. And as we age, we experience the lights beginning to dim, not unlike a dimmer on an overhead lamp. The Lord is so gracious that He gradually prepares

---

44 John Climacus, *The Ladder of Divine Ascent*, Step 6, "On Remembrance of Death" (Mahwah, NJ: Paulist Press, 1982), p. 133.

us for our eventual death. We Orthodox know that at our physical death, life begins.

We need to die to live. Our life is a series of small deaths and resurrections. In a sense, daily life is training for death. We experience many, many small deaths. For example, when we go to sleep at night, we lose it all. We lose our awareness, our possession of our mind, our memory, and our consciousness of our relationships. Sleep is a form of death. Awaking in the morning, though it may be slow, is a new day, a resurrection. I get up, pray, shower, brush my teeth, and eat breakfast. Perhaps the sun is shining, perhaps not. It's a new day, a new beginning.

My wife, who died decades ago, still lives. I talk to her every day. For her burial at St. Tikhon's Cemetery, there was a long cavalcade of cars on a cold February day, a rain-snow day. When we got to the cemetery, in a sense it was festive. Many priests and lay people surrounded the open grave. There were flowers, incense, and holy water to sprinkle on the casket. After the graveside service, we all went into the St. Tikhon's refectory to have a meal. The entire time was bittersweet. Then we drove home.

After we arrived home, I began to understand what had happened. Life now consisted of me and our two children, a daughter who was seventeen and a son who was eleven. They didn't have a mother, and I didn't have a wife. I was a man with two jobs and two children to raise. I felt hugely inadequate.

Forty days after the burial, I suggested to the children that we would have a little service at St. Vladimir's Chapel and then drive the two and a half hours to St. Tikhon's. The children said, "Okay, Dad." So we drove over to the cemetery. It happened to be raining that Friday afternoon. Because it was winter, the cemetery workers hadn't done anything to the gravesite. The flowers that were in bloom when my wife was buried were now dead but not removed. The mud atop the grave was raw, covered with heel marks, filled with rainwater. There were no other people at the cemetery that day.

As I stood and looked out, I saw a very pastoral scene with farmland, winding roads, and rolling hills. However, there was no movement. Not a cow or a person or a car moved on the landscape. Nothing stirred. All seemed dead.

The children and I stood under one umbrella. I could hear the raindrops on the umbrella cloth. The three of us felt quite sad. Then my son turned to me and asked, "Dad, what do you think Mom's face looks like now?" He wasn't being sarcastic. Rather, he was asking a sincere question about his dead mother. It was his mother's face he was asking about forty days after her death. He had seen enough movies to know the body decomposes. Of course, I did not answer the question. I gave him a hug and said, "I love you." That was sufficient.

In my head and heart was a bombardment of thoughts and temptations that sounded like, "Al, you believe all the Church teaches about death and resurrection. You believe in the Christian message about life after death. You believe that your wife is in a better place. Well, take a look, fella. There's no one here except the three of you. You have these two children to raise. You have no help." It was a great challenge to my faith. "You believe your wife is in a better place. Well, there isn't much evidence of it." In fact, the evidence was quite to the contrary. I felt blue, as the children did. So we said a prayer and went to get lunch.

That's death. Death is not nice. Death is not romantic. There is no sugarcoating the experience of the death of a loved one. We can't domesticate death. God did not create death. Christ did not experience death as a pleasant moment. No, death is death. As Metropolitan Anthony Bloom said in *Living Prayer*, "Death is death with all its tragic ugliness and monstrosity, and yet death ultimately is the only thing that gives us hope."[45]

We do know that the grave is a mystical door leading to new life. We try to ponder death as best we can. I'll be candid here. My wife is buried in a plot of ground for two people. The tombstone has a base and an upright. On the upright is a large inscription of our last name, Rossi. There are flowers carved in the stone, and a banner across that says, "Thy will be done." On the left side is a rectangle with her name, birth date, and death date. On the other side is a rectangle with my first name, birth date, and a blank for my death date.

I have a photo of the stone on my smartphone. With my phone I can spread my fingers and enlarge any part of the photo. I sometimes expand the grass on my side of the tombstone. I say

---

45 Anthony Bloom, *Living Prayer* (Springfield, IL: Templegate Publishers, 1996), p. 77.

to myself, "Hey, fella, now you are looking down on the grass. The day is going to come when you are looking up at that grass. That grass is going to cover you. That's the grass that already covers your wife." These thoughts might sound macabre and gloomy to some people. I would answer, "I don't think so." We need to realize that we are going to die and that God will take care of us.

St. John Climacus reminds us, "Just as bread is the most necessary of all foods, so the thought of death is the most essential of all works." He adds a touch of sanity by saying that the person who does not repent longs for death as a way out of life.[46]

So we remember death, but in no way seek death or look for deadly escapes from our God-given life. We remember death as a stimulus to live the present moment with great vigor, precisely because we are not dead yet.

> *Our life on earth is an experience of small deaths and resurrections.*

Our life on earth is an experience of small deaths and resurrections. Every loss is a gift God gives us so He can give us more life. He can close a door to open other doors. We might lose our keys or a tooth or a computer hard drive or some of our memory. We might lose loved ones through separation or death. Our

---

46 Climacus, *Ladder of Divine Ascent*, Step 6, "On Remembrance of Death," pp. 132-33.

reaction might be, "Ah, this is the beginning of the end." A more truthful thought would be, "This is the beginning of the beginning." It is. Every loss is the beginning of a new phase of our relationship with Christ, a fresh beginning toward our ultimate beginning—heaven.

The purpose of growing old is to prepare us to die. Not everyone gets the chance to grow old. I am old, in my seventies. The purpose of growing old isn't to get a hammock, have a large iced tea, and enjoy *la dolce vita*, the good life. No, no. We are here to live in Christ. That's what it is about. The grave leading to the door of a mystical new life is an opening. It is very difficult for us to understand, but we do the best we can.

The point is that we have a purpose on this planet until we die, regardless of our conditions or suffering. In our aging and suffering, we are an indefinable presence to others, a witness to where life really goes. In a word, we are a healing presence to others until our last breath.

I was with my wife when she died, and I am bold enough to say that I know what I hope I will say when the time comes for me to die. Frankly, this claim borders on arrogance. I know that I am a wimp and at my deathbed might collapse mentally and spiritually. We Orthodox believe the judgment doesn't consist of the Lord standing before us with a scroll, checking things off and tallying our behaviors, weighing our good and bad deeds. No, the judgment is a self-judgment. The Lord is going to say, in effect, "How did you do?" He is going to say to me, in effect,

"Al, I gave you a half-decent brain. How did you do publishing books and peer-reviewed articles?"

I will say, "Lord, have mercy."

He is likely to say, "Al, I gave you two children and three grandchildren. How did you do raising them into people after My image and likeness?"

I will reply, "Lord, have mercy."

He will say, "I gave you a bunch of seminarians to teach every semester for years and years. How did you do?"

I will say, "Lord, have mercy."

The Lord will then say, "Al, is that all you can say, 'Lord, have mercy?'"

I will answer, "Lord, have mercy."

And He will say, "Al, come in."

Of course, I don't know what I am going to say when I die. I am a coward. But I do know that God is good and gracious and wants us to ask for mercy. I also know that if we ask for mercy, we get mercy. No doubt about that.

I'll end this chapter with a quote from the beginning of the chapter about death. St. John Climacus said, "The fathers assert that perfect love is sinless, and it seems to me that a perfect sense of death is free from fear."

CHAPTER 9

Embracing Ambiguity

EMBRACING AMBIGUITY challenges our need to understand and control reality. After all, we are rational creatures with a God-given intellect.

When we begin to embrace ambiguity we become less rigid, less black-and-white in our thinking. We become softer. We become more kind.

The desert fathers understood ambiguity well, as the following story reveals:

> One day some of the brethren came to see Abba Anthony and among them was Abba Joseph. Wishing to test them, the old man mentioned a text from scripture. Starting with the youngest, he asked them what it meant. Each explained it as best he could. But to each one the old man said, "You have not yet found the answer."
>
> Last of all, he said to Abba Joseph, "And what do you think the text means?" He replied, "I do not know." Then Abba

Antony said, "Truly, Abba Joseph has found the way for he said, 'I do not know.'"[47]

In psychology, ambiguity is seen as "I don't know," and the metaphor is a circle drawn on the whiteboard. A professor draws a circle and asks, "What is that?" The students reply, "A circle." Then beside the circle she draws an incomplete circle. The question then is, "What is that?" Some people say, "That's an incomplete circle." Others say, "That's a circle." They see a circle closed even though it is not closed. That's the whole point. Some people need premature closure. They have difficulty saying, "I don't know."

Metropolitan Kallistos Ware says that it is not the task of Christianity to provide easy answers for every question, but to progressively make us aware of mystery. God is not so much the object of our knowledge as He is the cause of our awe.

That's very difficult for us because we are rational, and we do need an apologia for our faith. At the same time we need the ability to say, "I don't know. I'm willing to enter the mystery as best I can."

In theology, we use the word *apophatic*. In psychology we use the word *ambiguity*, which is not a perfect parallel, but it is good enough for our purposes. Both approaches emphasize "not knowing" as a way of knowing.

---

47 Benedicta Ward, trans., *The Sayings of the Desert Fathers* (Kalamazoo, MI: Cistercian Publications, 1975), p. 4.

When I was in graduate school for my doctorate in psychology, we were taught this sentence: "The sign of mental health is the ability to handle ambiguity." One way of assessing a person's ability to navigate the world—or to say that another way, to have a reasonable degree of stability and sanity—is to look at his or her ability to handle ambiguity. Ambiguity simply means, "I know that I don't know, and that's okay." It's okay to say, "I don't fully understand. I don't need cheap, quick answers."

Here's a little example of ambiguity from my son, Timothy, when he was three, four, and five. (This happened often.) I would say to my wife, "Honey, I think the family needs a little getaway vacation, a long weekend in Vermont, Thursday to Monday. I'll get the car all packed and have everything ready. I'll come home Thursday at five-thirty, and you just walk out the front door with the children. I won't even get out of the car. You just get in and we are out of here. Okay?"

> *A. I know that I don't know.*
>
> *B. I know that Christ knows.*
>
> *C. I trust Him.*

So on Thursday that would happen: I would pull up, my wife and children would get into the car, and off we'd go, from our home in New York to Vermont. We would not have traveled for half an hour when Timothy would ask, "Dad, how much longer until we get to Killington?"

I would answer, "Tim, I don't know. It's raining, and we are going to take a new road tonight, Route 17. So I just don't know."

Ten minutes later, with a little more stridency in his voice, he would ask, "Dad, how much longer?"

"Well, Tim, we haven't stopped for supper yet. I don't know when we are going to find a restaurant. So I just don't know."

Ten minutes later, with anger in his voice, he'd ask, "Dad, just tell me, how much longer."

I would retort, "Tim, we'll be there in four hours and twenty-two minutes."

He'd cheer up and say, "Thanks, Dad."

My answer had nothing to do with reality. Tim simply needed closure. He had a question; he wanted an answer. It didn't matter if it was true or false. He wanted any answer so that he could feel comfortable, so that he could escape the emotional pain of ambiguity. That's immaturity, which is appropriate for a three-, four-, or five-year-old. But it's not okay in an adult. So, for an adult with some maturity, a tolerance for ambiguity is translated as (a) I know that I don't know; (b) I know that Christ knows; (c) I trust Him. That's the beginning of mental health, sanity, sanctity.

St. Gregory of Nyssa said, "God's Name is not known. It is wondered at." So we continually try to move into the "wondering" of St. Gregory. When we begin to experience wonder, we begin to enter a new phase of awareness.

At St. Vladimir's Seminary, I have been graced by God with

the great honor of interacting with seminarians across many decades and have learned much from them. I have also discovered that learning is circular. We give and we get. We get and we give. I've also learned much about ambiguity from the seminarians, especially the married ones. For example, a seminarian comes who is married with children. He is taught, formed, and ordained. As graduation approaches, he isn't sure where the bishop will want him to go.

Frankly, the seminarians handle it rather gracefully, by and large. And I say to them, "How are you, given your level of ambiguity and not knowing where you are going?" They often say something like this: "Well, I certainly wish I knew where I was going. I would love to be able to plan for the schooling of my children and all the details of getting a moving van and all the rest. But I know this is happening for a purpose, and I know that God is trying to teach me to trust in Him more. So I am trying to do that."

Then I observe them going to classes and doing seminary things. And they have a bounce in their walk. They are light of foot, joyful—and this teaches *me*. The message is, "Al, you can learn to live better with ambiguity."

The Orthodox Church continues to unfold for us the sense of mystery, the sense of "I don't know." That is why, in the early Church, the Gospel of John was kept from the catechumens until they were baptized. It is the Gospel of high theology, high mystery. We move into the mystery of God slowly.

So saying "I don't know," being willing to live with ambiguity, is a sign of both psychological maturity and spiritual maturity.

Of course, not embracing ambiguity allows us to fall into theological fundamentalism. Fundamentalism says, in effect, "We have the answers and you don't." Fundamentalism is theological immaturity.

St. Gregory of Nyssa said, "God's Name is not known; it is wondered at."

On the day of my chrismation thirty-three years ago, my wife gave me a cross and chain with the inscribed words, "Together in deep silence." At the time, of course, she had no idea that the deep silence would include the chasm of her absence from this earth through an early death. Over the years I lost that cross. So for Christmas, I asked my daughter, Beth, to give me a new cross with the words "Together in deep silence." Beth gave me a little gold cross with those tiny words on the back. And I wear it with awe.

The three most important women in my life are embedded in that little gold cross. My daughter gave it to me, my wife's words are inscribed on it, and it is the cross my granddaughter, Kaitlyn, was baptized with. Yes, my daughter gave me her daughter's baptismal cross for Christmas. Needless to say, I cherish that cross. It embodies ambiguity for me. I know that I don't know why my wife had to die when the children were so young. I know that I don't know what the future holds for me. I don't know what the future holds for my children. But—and this is a big but—I do know that Christ knows all, and I try to trust Him.

Perhaps a great challenge to our rationality is to try to embrace the truth that we are, all of us, together in deep silence.

One thing is sure. I don't want to lose this cross. But Beth has already said, "Dad, if you lose the cross, it's okay. We'll get another one."

Stories of overcoming ambiguity can be found throughout the Bible. Strikingly,

> *Together in deep silence*

Jesus said as He hung on the Cross, "Father, forgive them, for they know not what they do." They certainly seemed like they knew what they were doing. They shouted, "His blood be upon us and upon our children." That's the point. Those at the foot of the Cross truly did not know what they were doing. So, too, with us. We just don't know, and that's okay, simply because that's the way it is. The more we know that we just don't know, the more we can try to rely on God.

When Jesus was asked by two of His apostles for specific places in His kingdom, He pointed out their lack of knowledge and their need to live within that ambiguity. He said, "You do not know what you are asking. Are you able to drink the cup that I am about to drink?" They replied, "We are able" (Matt.

20:22). Yet they had no idea how ambiguous the meaning of *cup* was and how their lives would unfold.

In another place Jesus said clearly, "What I am doing you do not understand now, but you will know after this" (John 13:7). And He gave unequivocal directives about living with ambiguity, such as "Watch therefore, for you know neither the day nor the hour" (Matt. 25:13). Couldn't be clearer.

Simple Honesty

AMBIGUITY CAN CREEP IN as we try to discern what to say to others about a problematic situation. How honest is honest?

I had an eye-opening moment when I heard a metropolitan say, "I never lie, but I have no responsibility to answer every question asked of me. " He was saying that he, and by extension the rest of us, simply need to be honest. Never lie, but don't say too much. Don't give TMI—too much information. Anyone can ask me any question, but that doesn't mean I will answer every question. I have no trouble answering some other question so the listener gets the truth, while not answering his or her question.

One time a teenage relative asked me why I was against homosexuals. I was stunned by the question. I know that I am not against homosexuals. I have dear friends who are same-sex attracted. But she asked the question and expected an answer.

I knew I couldn't answer the question as asked. So I

responded from a different perspective. I said, "I am for total freedom. I think that we humans are so free that we can actually choose whether or not to express our sexual desires sexually. I believe that sex is optional." That was a conversation stopper, and we talked about something else. But she asked a question that I was not going to play into and try to answer. We never lie, but we don't say more than is truthful or necessary.

After my wife died, I took my children to visit my mother-in-law, Bubba, for a week every year. Bubba loved to play cards—specifically, 500 Rummy—as a way of spending time with us. I am not fond of playing cards, but every evening the four of us played 500 Rummy until midnight, or so it seemed. One game ended and another began.

Late one evening I was dealt a perfect hand. I said softly, "If I were the three of you, I would lay down whatever cards I could, because I am going out when my turn comes."

Bubba said nicely, "Al, you're lying."

Without missing a beat, my eleven-year-old son, Timothy, said, "Bubba, my dad never lies."

The game went on and, yes, I did go out when my turn came. And I'll never forget Tim's comment. He did not need to say what he did. You see, I had included my children in my effort to overcome my tendency to exaggerate and sometimes lie by asking them to correct me when I did. Over the years, the children did just that, saying such things as, "Dad, the fish you caught wasn't as big as you are saying."

We need to never lie and we need to include others in our attempts to be honest. Interestingly, as an adult, Timothy adopted the same strategy. He asked his wife to correct him if he ever lied. In a conversation with her twin sister, Timothy's wife simply said, "Tim never lies." She could say that because she was part of helping him speak the truth.

We really don't know much about ourselves. We don't know much about the truth of our past. My wife and I were married in a Roman Catholic ceremony, mostly to please my parents. My wife gradually began to go to Orthodox services, the religion of her childhood. I went with her but didn't convert for about five years.

Did I take too long to convert? Would the family and I have been stronger if I had converted earlier? I don't know. And that's okay. I know that I don't know. I know that God knows. I try to trust Him.

The past is what it is. We can't change it. Someone said that repentance is giving up all hope of a better past—that is, the short-term and the long-term past. But we don't have to have a self-righteous attitude, telling ourselves that everything we did was proper, correct, and the best we could do. All we can do is pray for God's mercy and let go of the past.

We also often don't know what is best in the present moment. We pray, ask for guidance, and can easily be surprised at how dense we are and how judgmental of others we can be. In the present moment, I may not know if God wants me to plan a family outing for next week or use the time to prepare my classes.

Regarding the future, it's a no-brainer that there is nothing we can be certain about. We might not get a next breath; we might have no future. But, as humans, we are sorely tempted to worry about future events. Lord, have mercy, and He does.

About Others

WE KNOW THAT WE DON'T KNOW why others do what they do. There is an entire universe of reasons people behave as they do. Why is this person pushing ahead of me in the checkout line? Why wasn't I asked to be a chaperone for the youth group? Why was the cashier obnoxious when I asked for a receipt? Truth be told, I don't know. There may be very good reasons for the rude behaviors. Perhaps the obnoxious person just got a phone call from her doctor, saying a serious blood test turned out positive and she needs to visit the hospital for an operation. Perhaps the person is suffering from abdominal pain but wants to work as much as he can to make money for his family. We just don't know. However, we are often sorely tempted to infer motives in others because we think we know best.

The way out of ambiguity is continual prayer, saying the name of Jesus over and over. St. Hesychius said, "The more the rain pours down upon earth, the more it softens the earth; so too the holy name of Christ, the more we call upon it, the more it softens the earth of our heart, and fills it with joy and delight."

Ambiguity is all about loss of control. Control is a defense mechanism against immaturity and fear. We fear the things we are not mature enough to handle.

What can we expect if we try to be more open to a sense of ambiguity? Initially we will likely be hit with confusion and despondency. Abba Poemen said, "Acedia [despondency] is there every time one begins something, and there is no worse passion, but if a man recognizes it for what it is, he will gain peace."

Ambiguity is similar to cognitive dissonance. Cognitive dissonance is disharmony between differing thoughts or between thoughts and behaviors. I am reminded of an Alaskan seminarian who attended St. Vladimir's years ago. He had cognitive dissonance because he knew God wanted him to be at seminary, but he couldn't stand the warm weather. One day a faculty member opened the door of the walk-in refrigerator in the kitchen, and sitting inside, reading a book, was the Alaskan student. The faculty member asked what he was doing. He said he wanted to be in a place that felt like home. He had reduced his dissonance by changing his behavior.

Embracing ambiguity requires an attitude adjustment. We need to drop our mental burdens and "cast our burdens on the Lord."

Conclusion

BECOMING A HEALING PRESENCE is within range for each of us. When I was a child, my mentally challenged Uncle Martin lived in our home. He often got down on his hands and knees and let me ride on his back around the house. I was the cowboy riding on his horse's back. His nickname for me was Willy.

The most responsible job he ever held was as a night watchman at a fruit stand. Uncle Martin would have given all the fruit to needy people, or even thieves, for that matter. That is who he was.

Most of the day he sat in a chair, watching TV, never changing the channel. When anyone walked by and asked how he was doing, he would say, "What's a fella gonna do?" To this day, decades after his death, many people, including me, quote Uncle Martin. He left a fingerprint on everyone he met, leaving them stronger and with more hope.

God gave Uncle Martin below-average intelligence, but he

used his God-given abilities, meager as they may seem to some, to be an above-average healing presence to others.

"Becoming a healing presence" is a code phrase for loving others as best we can. It is code for actively listening to others, intuiting their needs, and serving them in whatever way we can.

We become a healing presence because Christ is the healing Presence through us. He is "all in all" through us to others. We can't give what we don't have. We can't give Christ's healing presence to others if we are not intimate with Him ourselves. We grow in intimacy with Him through stillness and prayer.

St. Theophan said that the essence of the Christian life is to keep the mind in the heart before God. Christ moves through us as a healing fire to the extent that we allow ourselves to be open and available to Him. We need to spend quiet time with Him, gently speaking His name or saying the Jesus Prayer, and we need to do all we can to have conscious contact with Him all day and when we awake during the night.

Becoming a healing presence is a simple process. All we have to do is do what we can. As St. Irenaeus said, "We need to relax in God's hands." My Uncle Martin's statement, "What's a fella gonna do?" can be a relaxed way to allow Christ to do through us what we cannot do for ourselves.

Yes, it is a simple process, but because we are human and complicated, it is both simple and difficult. May He live in and through us now.

About the Author

Dr. Albert S. Rossi is a licensed clinical psychologist and Christian educator who has spoken and written widely on these topics. Dr. Rossi was a member of the SCOBA Commission on Contemporary Social and Moral Issues for six years. He is currently Director of Field Education and serves as the resident clinical psychologist at St. Vladimir's Seminary. He hosts the podcast *Becoming a Healing Presence* on Ancient Faith Radio.

Listen to Dr. Rossi's podcast at

http://www.ancientfaith.com/podcasts/healingpresence

More Books

FROM ANCIENT FAITH PUBLISHING

The Morning Offering: Daily Thoughts for Orthodox Christians

Abbot Tryphon

Thousands of readers and listeners have benefited from the fatherly wisdom and insight of The Morning Offering, the blog and podcast of Abbot Tryphon of All-Merciful Saviour Monastery, Vashon Island, Washington. Now Abbot Tryphon's reflections on faith and contemporary life have been collected in book form, with one entry for each day of the year. Start your day with The Morning Offering and keep yourself oriented toward Christ all through the day.

Thirty Steps to Heaven: The Ladder of Divine Ascent for All Walks of Life

Vassilios Papavassiliou

Many laypeople have attempted to read the great spiritual classic, The Ladder of Divine Ascent, but have been frustrated in attempting to apply the lessons of this monastic text to their everyday lives in the world. In Thirty Steps, Archimandrite Vassilios interprets the Ladder for the ordinary Christian without sacrificing any of its beauty and power. Now you too can accept the challenge offered by St. John Climacus to ascend closer to God with each passing day.

An Introduction to God: Encountering the Divine in Orthodox Christianity
Andrew Stephen Damick

Speaking to non-believers and believers alike, Fr. Andrew Damick attempts to create a sacred space in which we can encounter God. In this compact volume, he distills the essence of the traditional Christian faith, addressing the fundamental mysteries of where God is, who God is, why we go to church, and why Christian morality matters. If you've only heard about the Protestant or Roman Catholic version of Christianity, what he has to say may surprise you—and make you long to encounter God in Jesus Christ.

Fire from Ashes: The Reality of Perpetual Conversion
Joseph Huneycutt and Steve Robinson

Popular bloggers and podcasters Fr. Joseph Huneycutt and Steve "the Builder" Robinson explore the reality of life in Christ as perpetual conversion—falling and rising, falling and rising again. No matter how cold the ashes of our hearts, with Christ's help we can fan them back into flame. Illustrated with Steve's inimitable cartoons.

Help! I'm Bored in Church: Entering Fully into the Divine Liturgy
David R. Smith

Do you ever find yourself feeling bored in church? Don't despair—you're not alone, and there is hope! Fr. David Smith offers four compelling reasons for going to church regardless of how we feel. This book will help you see church as the best place you could possibly be—and the place you most want to be.

Words for Our Time: The Spiritual Words of Matthew the Poor, vol. 1

The twentieth-century elder Abba Matta of Egypt, known in the West as Matthew the Poor, is widely regarded as the greatest Egyptian elder since St. Antony the Great. He produced a huge and varied body of work in Arabic, only a little of which has been translated into English. In addition, a great many of his informal talks to monks and visitors were recorded. This volume is the first appearance in English of a small selection of these talks.

Abba Matta had a marvelous ability to communicate the deepest spiritual truths in the simplest and most practical language, making them accessible to laypeople as well as monastics. He speaks to the heart rather than the head, gently exhorting the reader to pursue a deeper life in Christ. To read these talks is to sit at the feet of one of the greatest spiritual teachers of our age.

The Scent of Holiness: Lessons from a Women's Monastery
Constantina Palmer
Every monastery exudes the scent of holiness, but women's monasteries have their own special flavor. Join Constantina Palmer as she makes frequent pilgrimages to a women's monastery in Greece and absorbs the nuns' particular approach to their spiritual life. If you're a woman who's read of Mount Athos and longed to partake of its grace-filled atmosphere, this book is for you. Men who wish to understand how women's spirituality differs from their own will find it a fascinating read as well.

Podcasts

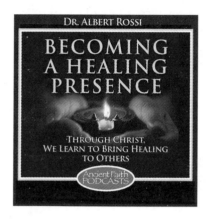

We are a healing presence to others when we give them strength and when we give them hope. Dr. Albert Rossi explains how to do both in imitation of Christ, our complete healer, who desires nothing more than for us to be His humanity on earth—his healing presence to others.

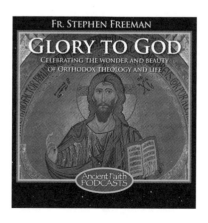

Fr. Stephen Freeman's blog, *Glory to God for all Things,* has quickly become one of the most-read Orthodox sites on the web, being translated frequently into Romanian, French, and Serbian by enthusiastic readers. He is also the author of the Ancient Faith Publishing book *Everywhere Present.*

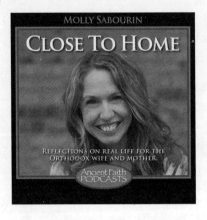

Molly Sabourin is a freelance writer focusing on issues of family, faith, and community. She is also an Orthodox Christian, blogger, wife, and a frenzied mother of four.

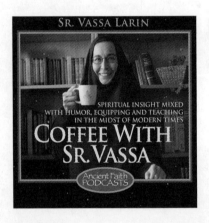

Coffee with Sister Vassa is a brief weekly program hosted by Sr. Dr. Vassa Larin, a nun of the Russian Orthodox Church Abroad and liturgiologist of the University of Vienna in Austria. The program offers an engaging reflection on the Orthodox Church calendar of the current week, including the lives of the saints, scriptural passages, and the Orthodox liturgical tradition, along with a light dose of humor.